"Fears, phobias, and even excessive use of drugs and alcohol can be fuelled by people's fears of feeling anxious or uncomfortable. Watt and Stewart teach readers to confront their discomfort and fear head-on rather than constantly fight these feelings. The strategies described in the book are based on sound scientific research. Anyone whose biggest fear is fear itself should read this book!"

—Martin M. Antony, Ph.D., ABPP, professor of psychology at Ryerson University in Toronto, ON, Canada, and author of *The Shyness and Social Anxiety Workbook*

"Watt and Stewart have produced an important, timely, and clinically meaningful volume addressing the fear of fear. Their book is highly logical, linear, and clear in its presentation. The case vignettes help illustrate the role of fear of fear in the day-to-day lives of people and show how it can impact their lives. The clinical intervention strategies are steeped in evidence-based theory and are easy to understand and follow. Overall, there can be no doubt that this book will be an instrumental resource for researchers, teachers, clinicians, and the general public."

—Michael J. Zvolensky, Ph.D., Richard and Pamela Ader Green and Gold Distinguished Full Professor in the department of psychology at the University of Vermont and director of the Anxiety and Health Research Laboratory and Clinic

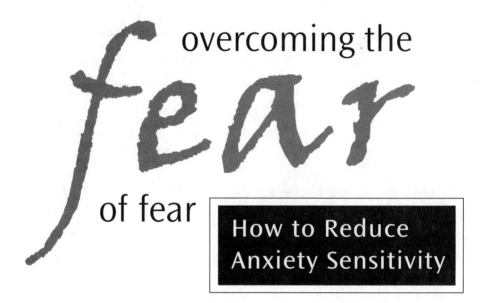

overcoming the

fear

of fear

How to Reduce Anxiety Sensitivity

Margo C. Watt, Ph.D. &
Sherry H. Stewart, Ph.D.

New Harbinger Publications, Inc.

Publisher's Note

Distributed in Canada by Raincoast Books

Copyright © 2008 by Margo C. Watt & Sherry H. Stewart
New Harbinger Publications, Inc.
5674 Shattuck Avenue
Oakland, CA 94609
www.newharbinger.com

FSC
Mixed Sources
Product group from well-managed
forests and other controlled sources

Cert no. SW-COC-002283
www.fsc.org
© 1996 Forest Stewardship Council

All Rights Reserved
Printed in the United States of America

Acquired by Tesilya Hanauer; Cover design by Amy Shoup;
Edited by Nelda Street

Library of Congress Cataloging-in-Publication Data
Watt, Margo C.
 Overcoming the fear of fear : how to reduce anxiety sensitivity / Margo C. Watt and Sherry H. Stewart ; foreword by Steven Taylor.
    p. cm.
 Includes bibliographical references.
 ISBN-13: 978-1-57224-558-7 (pbk. : alk. paper)
 ISBN-10: 1-57224-558-1 (pbk. : alk. paper)
1.   Anxiety sensitivity--Popular works. 2.   Anxiety sensitivity--Treatment--Popular works. I. Stewart, Sherry H. II. Title.
 RC531.W38 2008
 616.85'223--dc22

                                    2008039800

10 09 08
10 9 8 7 6 5 4 3 2 1   First printing

The thing I fear most is fear.

—Michel de Montaigne

Contents

PART III
How to Reduce Anxiety Sensitivity

PART IV
Preventing Relapse

Foreword

The notion of fear-of-fear is familiar to most people today. It famously entered into popular consciousness in 1933 with Franklin D. Roosevelt's inaugural address, in which he said, "The only thing we have to fear is fear itself—nameless, unreasoning, unjustified terror which paralyzes needed efforts to convert retreat into advance" (Rosenman 1938, 11). Scholars knew about fear-of-fear centuries before Roosevelt's speech. Perhaps the earliest reference was by Michel de Montaigne, who remarked in a paragraph consisting of a single sentence, "The thing I fear most is fear" (1580, 53). Unfortunately, this was all de Montaigne had to say on the subject. In the centuries to follow, references to fear-of-fear continued to be made by scholars. Yet it was not until the 1980s that scientists began asking important questions about this concept: What exactly is fear-of-fear? What causes it? Is excessive fear-of-fear an important problem for some people? If so, how do we help them overcome it?

Among the most important pioneers in this field were Steven Reiss and Richard J. McNally, who set about answering some of these important questions (see for example Reiss and McNally 1985). Instead of using the popular term *fear-of-fear*, which can mean many different things to different people, Reiss and McNally precisely defined the concept, which they called *anxiety sensitivity* (AS). This is the fear of anxiety-related bodily sensations, arising from the person's beliefs about the dangerousness of the sensations. Bodily sensations associated with anxiety include rapid heartbeat, sweating, trembling, dizziness, and concentration difficulties. Reiss and McNally proposed that people differ in their levels of AS. Some people have little or no AS, some people have extremely high levels, and some have moderate levels. People with high levels of AS tend to be very frightened of anxiety-related sensations. If they experience rapid heartbeat, they are likely to believe that they are going to die of a heart attack. If they sweat or tremble in public, they are likely to worry that people will reject or ridicule them. If they have trouble concentrating because they are anxious, they worry that their concentration difficulties will lead to insanity.

Reiss and McNally developed the first comprehensive theory of AS and developed ways of measuring a person's level of AS. Other researchers soon recognized the importance of Reiss and McNally's work, and hundreds of studies have since been published on AS. The research suggested that a person's level of AS is largely learned as a result of childhood and other experiences, although genes also have a modest impact (Taylor et al. 2008). Research also indicates that high levels of AS are common in the general population, and that high AS increases the person's risk of developing all kinds of psychological problems, including anxiety disorders, problems with alcohol or drug abuse, and problems with chronic pain or excessive worry about one's health. Research also indicates that a particular form of cognitive behavioral therapy can reduce AS and thereby help the person overcome anxiety disorders or related problems. These important research findings are discussed in this book.

The authors of this book, Margo Watt and Sherry Stewart, are psychologists who have conducted a good deal of important research on AS. Equally important, they are skilled clinicians who are experienced in using cognitive behavioral therapy to treat people suffering from excessive AS. In this book, Watt and Stewart explain the nature of AS and present readers with the most important research findings. The authors clearly explain why elevated AS is an important problem that needs to be corrected, and they describe a number of scientifically proven cognitive behavioral methods to help people overcome excessive AS. This is the first self-help book devoted specifically to overcoming problems associated with elevated AS. Given that elevated AS appears to play a role in so many different clinical problems, the exercises described in this book should be helpful for many people suffering from emotional and other problems, especially if they are using this book while consulting a mental health professional with expertise in cognitive behavioral therapy. This book is also a valuable aid for trainees in the mental health professions, who will be able to consult this concise, lucid, and well-illustrated book in order to learn how to effectively treat people suffering from excessive AS. Drs. Watt and Stewart are to be congratulated for producing such a valuable resource for both consumers and mental health practitioners.

Steven Taylor, Ph.D., ABPP
Professor, Department of Psychiatry
University of British Columbia

Acknowledgments

This book and the research project upon which it is based would not have been possible without the assistance of a number of individuals. First and foremost, we would like to thank Dr. Patricia J. Conrod, a BPS Chartered Clinical Psychologist and Clinical Lecturer in the Department of Psychological Medicine and Psychiatry at King's College, London, UK. The treatment manual for the brief cognitive behavioral treatment (CBT) was adapted in part from previous interventions conducted by Dr. Conrod and colleagues (Conrod 2000; Conrod, Stewart, Pihl, Cote, Fontaine, and Dongier, 2000). Credit also is due to the seminal work of other researchers including Dr. David Barlow at Boston University and Dr. Michelle Craske at the University of California, Los Angeles, as well as Patrick J. Harrington and Michael J. Telch (1994) at the University of Texas at Austin.

The authors are indebted to the following graduate students from Dalhousie University's Clinical Psychology PhD program who delivered the intervention over the past five years: Cheryl Birch, Denise Bernier, Marie-josée Lefaivre, Lindsay Uman, Brigitte Sabourin, and Kerry MacSwain; as well as Dr. Kim Mac Lean, a faculty member in the Department of Psychology at St. Francis Xavier University. Over the years, a number of student research assistants at both sites have provided valuable support for the project. At St. Francis Xavier, these individuals included Tara MacDonald, Lesley Terry, Sarah Oulton, Emma MacDonald, Cathy Hilchey, and Hayley Russell. At Dalhousie, these individuals included Heather Lee Loughlin, Ellen Rhyno, Jennifer Theakston, Adrienne Girling, Dee Gavric, and Maureen Balcom. Thanks to Cathy Hilchey, who provided the art work on page 78.

The authors are grateful to the following funding agencies, without whose generous support this research would not have been possible. Thanks to St. Francis Xavier University, which provided funding for the pilot study via a Canadian Institutes of Health Research (CIHR) Seed Grant. Thanks to Nova Scotia Health Research Foundation (NSHRF), which provided financial support for the project from 2003 through 2006, and thanks to the Sport Canada Research Initiative (SCRI) for its current support.

Finally, the authors extend a sincere thank you to the many under-graduate students at both St. Francis Xavier and Dalhousie Universities who participated in the brief CBT and, thus, made an important con-tribution to the research literature and clinical practice in the area of anxiety and related problems.

Introduction

Fear is only as deep as the mind allows.

—Japanese proverb

We all experience fear. Fear is what we feel when we encounter a bear in the woods, sit through turbulence on an airplane, or hear a strange noise late at night when we are all alone. Anxiety, on the other hand, is what we experience when we think about possibly encountering a bear in the woods, anticipate air turbulence on an upcoming flight, or worry about being alone at night. Related to fear and anxiety is anxiety sensitivity. *Anxiety sensitivity* refers to the tendency to respond fearfully to the bodily sensations associated with fear and anxiety. Such bodily sensations include a racing heartbeat, fast breathing, and sweating. In other words, anxiety sensitivity is the fear of fear.

As the Japanese proverb above suggests, anxiety sensitivity involves a particular way of thinking, or a "cognitive style." The cognitive style characterizing anxiety sensitivity involves *catastrophizing* (thinking the worst) about the consequences of anxiety sensations. For example, if you have anxiety sensitivity, you might fear a racing heartbeat, believing that it means you're about to have a heart attack. You might fear dizziness because you think you're having a mental breakdown ("going crazy"). You might fear the trembling sensations you have when anticipating being embarrassed in front of other people. In contrast, a person with low anxiety sensitivity would consider such sensations to be unpleasant, but fleeting and harmless, consequences of being in an anxious state.

High levels of anxiety sensitivity are associated with various types of mental and physical health problems, including panic attacks, substance abuse, and pain. We'll look at the role anxiety sensitivity plays in development and persistence of these problems later in this book.

As authors, we intend for this book to introduce you to the concept of anxiety sensitivity. This book is also designed to familiarize you with the research findings that inform our understanding of this important risk factor for anxiety and related disorders. This book is further intended to help you determine whether you have high levels of anxiety sensitivity and to offer suggestions as to what you can do about it. We will introduce you to techniques (targeting both thinking patterns and actions) that can reduce your tendency to respond anxiously to fearful situations. Finally, the book discusses possible changes in lifestyle that may help you better manage your anxiety sensitivity.

The organization of this book reflects the organization of a brief treatment program targeted at changing faulty ways of thinking and acting (that is, a *cognitive behavioral* treatment), which research has shown are involved in causing and perpetuating anxiety sensitivity. We designed this program to specifically target high levels of anxiety sensitivity. Our research over the past three years has shown that this program is effective at reducing anxiety sensitivity levels and thus reducing pain-related anxiety (Watt et al. 2006b), depressed mood (Watt, Stewart, and Bernier 2005), and problems associated with drinking alcohol (Watt et al. 2006a). You will get the most benefit from the book by reading the chapters in order. Nonetheless, we've structured each chapter to stand on its own so you can focus on the sections that are most relevant to you.

Part I of this book begins with a definition of anxiety sensitivity and a description of what we know about why some people have higher levels of "fear of fear" than others. We offer an overview of how anxiety sensitivity is measured and then invite you to assess your own level of anxiety sensitivity.

Part II explains why anxiety sensitivity is important to our understanding and treatment of anxiety and related disorders. In this section, we examine the role of anxiety sensitivity in contributing to the development and maintenance of anxiety-related disorders, including panic disorder, post-traumatic stress disorder, and social phobia. We also examine the role of anxiety sensitivity in initiating and perpetuating other mental and physical health problems, such as health anxiety (or *hypochondriasis*), chronic pain, substance abuse, and depression.

In Part III, we turn our attention to how you can reduce anxiety sensitivity by changing your thoughts, actions, and lifestyle. Here, we'll discuss ways of thinking that can fuel anxiety (for example, catastrophizing about the consequences of bodily sensations and overestimating the probability that these consequences will happen). We'll examine ways of behaving—both harmful and helpful—that can keep you trapped in, or release you from, anxiety-elevating patterns. We'll review how making lifestyle changes, particularly increasing physical activity, can help you better manage or even eliminate your "fear of fear."

Finally, in Part IV, we talk about *relapse prevention*, how to maintain the gains you achieve by acquiring and practicing skills for managing and reducing your anxiety sensitivity. Here, we'll review how to practice your skills, how to prepare to react when you slip back into old ways of thinking and acting, and how to persevere with habit changes.

A self-help book is intended as a tool, and a tool is most useful when well suited to the task at hand. A self-help book is not intended to replace professional (medical or psychological) help. Indeed, you may need to complete the program described herein with the assistance of a professional. If you're someone whose functioning at work, home, or in relationships is impaired by mental and physical health problems associated with high levels of anxiety sensitivity (such as panic attacks, substance abuse, and pain-related anxiety), then we advise consultation with a professional. If you're someone with high levels of anxiety sensitivity but a limited support system, then working with a professional could enhance the benefits to be derived from this book.

In an empirical examination of some of the top-selling self-help books, R. E. Redding and colleagues (forthcoming) concluded that a good self-help book should be (1) clearly focused on the topic and (2) solidly grounded in research (with appropriate references, bibliographies, and lists of resources for further study and comparison); (3) the authors should be well qualified in training and experience to write about the topic; and (4) there should be some evidence that the book has "worked" (that is, other people have found it useful in their lives). Before releasing this book, through careful research we ensured that the program on which the book is based effectively helps people with high anxiety sensitivity. As mentioned previously, our research over the past three years has shown that this program is effective at reducing high anxiety sensitivity and associated problems. Moreover, other research (Baillie and Rapee 2004) has found that cognitive behavioral treatments delivered in a self-help format similar to the one used here can work for many of the anxiety-related disorders. We're confident that the program described in this book will translate into an effective self-help program for some and will serve as a helpful manual for use with the assistance of a trained therapist for others. We hope you'll find that this book works for you.

THE AUTHORS

Dr. Watt has a doctorate degree in clinical psychology. She has conducted research, published, taught, and practiced in the area of anxiety and related disorders for over ten years. She is an associate professor of psychology at St. Francis Xavier University in Antigonish, Nova Scotia, and an adjunct professor of psychology at Dalhousie University in Halifax, Nova Scotia. Her research interests include investigating and treating anxiety-related disorders, including health anxiety and pain, and cognitive behavioral therapy (CBT) approaches to treatment. Dr. Watt maintains a limited clinical practice wherein she treats patients with anxiety and pain-related disorders.

Dr. Stewart has a doctorate degree in clinical psychology and has conducted research, taught, and practiced in the area of anxiety and related disorders for over fifteen years. She has gained an international reputation for her research in the areas of addictions, anxiety disorders, and the comorbidity of mental health and substance abuse disorders. In particular, she has gained national and international recognition for her important health-related research on a novel approach to preventing alcohol abuse in adolescents and for her innovations in addictions research. In a recent survey of faculty members within clinical psychology programs accredited by the American Psychological Association, Dr. Stewart ranked nineteenth out of the seventy most productive faculty in terms of total publications and peer-reviewed journal articles (Stewart, Wu, and Roberts 2007). She is a professor of psychiatry and psychology at Dalhousie University in Halifax, Nova Scotia, and has a cross-appointment in the Department of Community Health and Epidemiology at Dalhousie. She maintained a clinical practice in Halifax, Nova Scotia, for a number of years.

Part I

What Is Anxiety Sensitivity?

chapter 1

Understanding Anxiety Sensitivity

Learning to know anxiety is an adventure which every man has to affront if he would not go to perdition either by not having known anxiety or by sinking under it. He therefore who has learned rightly to be in anxiety has learned the most important thing.

—Søren Kierkegaard

Kierkegaard's quote suggests that, to avoid being overwhelmed by anxiety, we must learn to be "in anxiety." This book is designed to do just that, to help people, in particular those who have a high level of anxiety sensitivity, learn to feel anxiety and not "sink under it." This chapter introduces the concept of anxiety sensitivity and explains the relationship among fear, anxiety, panic, and anxiety sensitivity. You'll learn how our bodies normally respond to stress (our natural emergency response system) and how some people are hypersensitive to the sensations produced by this response system. You'll be introduced to the types of concerns that bother people with high anxiety sensitivity.

Case Vignette: Isabel

Isabel is a twenty-three-year-old woman, who, for as long as she can remember, has been prone to bouts of anxiety. As a child, she remembers being particularly frightened by the sensations associated with anxiety, such as stomachaches. As a teenager, she dreaded gym classes because the sensations evoked by the physical activity—increased respiration, perspiration, and heart rate—frightened her. Whenever her heart started racing and she started to sweat, she was filled with a sense of dread that something terrible would happen to her. Isabel feared that she might have a heart attack or something worse—like completely losing control of herself. Moreover, she feared that if the other students noticed her anxiety, they'd tease her and make fun of her. Whenever her mother had asked Isabel to help her carry groceries up the stairs to their apartment, Isabel had made excuses to avoid the risk of having the feared sensations. In her teenage years, Isabel started to experience panic attacks, acute episodes of sudden and intense anxiety that seemingly came on completely out of the blue. These attacks occurred two or three times a month; sometimes she'd wake up in the middle of the night in the throes of a panic attack. When she wasn't having a panic attack, she worried about having one. She started to avoid situations or events that she thought might lead to a panic attack. By her second year in college, her panic attacks were so bad that she sought help at the campus health and counseling center.

Isabel has panic disorder. Panic disorder is one type of anxiety disorder that is characterized by unexpected and repeated episodes of intense fear. This fear is accompanied by a number of physical symptoms that may include chest pain, heart palpitations, shortness of breath, dizziness, or abdominal distress. The exact cause or causes of panic disorder are unknown and are the subject of intense scientific investigation. Heredity, other biological factors, and stressful life events are all believed to play a role in the onset of panic disorder. Another factor known to play a role in causing panic disorder is a high level of anxiety sensitivity.

Anxiety sensitivity (AS) refers to the fear of sensations associated with being in an "aroused" state, such as being anxious or distressed. Fear of these sensations arises from the belief that these sensations signify that harmful consequences will follow. Isabel, for example, was frightened by the sensation of her heart's racing; she feared that something terrible would happen, like a heart attack. Having high AS means that Isabel is predisposed to misinterpreting and catastrophizing about body sensations associated with being anxious. Having high AS increases Isabel's risk of developing panic disorder. Isabel is not alone. Studies tend to show that 10 to 20 percent of people in the general population have elevated levels of anxiety sensitivity (Bernstein et al. 2006; Watt, Stewart, and Cox 1998). These individuals may fear breathing difficulties, thinking that they signify an asthma attack; fear that feelings of detachment and being spacey indicate that they're going crazy; or fear that blushing while anxious will draw unwanted attention and ridicule from others. In other words, these people fear their own fears. This additional fear puts them at risk for a lot of problems, which we'll discuss shortly. First, let's review some related concepts to thoroughly explain what anxiety sensitivity is (and what it is not) and why we need to understand it better.

DISTINGUISHING BETWEEN FEAR AND ANXIETY

Fear sharpens the senses; anxiety paralyzes them.

—German psychiatrist Kurt Goldstein

Everyone has experienced fear and anxiety. Seeing a scary movie, barely avoiding a car accident, walking down a dark alleyway, meeting a bear in the woods—all can elicit feelings of fear and anxiety, resulting in weak knees, pounding heart, shortness of breath, and racing mind. We often use the words "fear" and "anxiety" interchangeably, but they're not simply different labels for the same emotion. On one hand, fear is defined as an emotional state in the presence of a dangerous or unpleasant stimulus. Typically fear is accompanied by an internal, subjective experience of extreme agitation, a desire to flee or attack, as were a variety of arousal sensations (*The Penguin Dictionary of Psychology*, 3rd ed., s.v. "fear"). Whereas fear is a response to a current threat, anxiety is oriented toward the future. In short, fear is a reaction to a somewhat clear and present danger; anxiety is a reaction to an anticipated situation or event in the future.

It's good that we experience fear and anxiety; otherwise, we'd be at risk for harm. Fear is our reaction to an identified threat (we meet the bear); anxiety is our body's response to perceived threat (we anticipate meeting the bear in the near future). Anxiety is the body's way of telling us to prepare for *fight or flight*, a response controlled by our autonomic nervous system (ANS). The ANS regulates many of the major muscles and organs of the body, such as the heart, stomach, and intestines. Most of the time, we're unaware of the ANS, because it operates involuntarily and reflexively. We do, however, notice the operation of the ANS in an emergency because we breathe faster, our heart rate rises, and we start to sweat. For our ancestors, this response was vital for survival; for us, it remains a reaction to stressful situations when we feel threatened. For example, most of us would react with alarm if we encountered a bear while walking in the woods. Our sense of alarm might include an increased heart rate, increased sweating and respiration, dizziness, nausea, and difficulty concentrating. This response prepares the body to act quickly, depending on how we appraise the degree of risk and the action to take.

Of course, we also react with alarm to things that do not necessarily involve a physical threat. Taking a test, making a speech, or performing in front of others also can evoke the same sensations as seeing a bear. All of these situations produce physical sensations, such as nausea, dizziness, shortness of breath, and racing heart. Some people become anxious about the physical sensations themselves. These people (about 19 percent of women and 10 percent of men; Bernstein et al. 2007; Stewart, Taylor, and Baker 1997) are said to have high AS. When highly anxiety-sensitive people experience bodily sensations associated with anxiety, they tend to amplify, or "turn up the volume" on, these sensations; they focus on the sensations, misinterpret their meaning, and begin to catastrophize about what they mean. In contrast, less-anxiety-sensitive individuals tend to reduce the volume, recognizing these sensations to be normal, temporary, and unpleasant but otherwise harmless consequences of being in an anxious state (Reiss 1991).

In short, fear is what we experience when we encounter the bear in the woods, anxiety is what we experience when we think about encountering a bear in the woods in the near future, and anxiety sensitivity is the fear of the consequences of the sensations we experience when we encounter the bear or even think about encountering the bear. First, there's fear, and then there's fear of fear.

WHEN IS ANXIETY A PROBLEM?

Anxiety is a natural emotion that every single person experiences. It's part of being human. Some people, however, experience anxiety more often or more intensely than others. Anxiety is not always bad. In some situations, being anxious may be appropriate or even desirable. For example, if you're preparing for a tennis match or a piano recital, having some anxiety will actually enhance your performance. This is known as the Yerkes-Dodson law, after Robert Yerkes and John Dodson (1908), who first observed that too little or too much arousal can interfere with performance and that a moderate level of arousal is best for maximum performance in a task. Anxiety can vary in severity, from mild uneasiness to extreme distress; it also can vary in frequency, from occasional distress to seemingly constant unease. But when you experience anxiety as recurrent abrupt episodes of intense fear or discomfort (panic attacks), persistent concerns about having more attacks and the potential consequences of those attacks, and a significant change in behavior related to the attacks (escape and avoidance behavior), then it can interfere with your daily life and meet the criteria for panic disorder, as outlined in the diagnostic manual of the American Psychiatric Association (DSM-IV-TR 2000).

WHAT KINDS OF SITUATIONS MAKE YOU ANXIOUS?

Please check off the situations that apply to you.

_____ Speaking in public

_____ Participating in groups

_____ Walking up stairs or hills

_____ Darkness

_____ Being alone

_____ Getting really angry

_____ Being in closed spaces (such as elevators or cars with the windows rolled up)

_____ Other things _____

HOW DO YOU FEEL WHEN YOU'RE ANXIOUS?

Please check off the situations that apply to you.

_____ Heart racing or fluttering

_____ Rapid breathing

_____ Head aching

_____ Choking or suffocating

_____ Chest pains

_____ Sweating

_____ Dizziness

_____ Other sensations _____

WHAT IS PANIC?

Research shows that panic is more than just an extreme form of anxiety. In some ways, the two are distinct emotional experiences. Anxiety is accompanied by apprehension, worry, and tension; panic is accompanied by strong autonomic arousal (racing heart, increased respiration, and sweating), extreme fear, and urges to fight or flee (Barlow 1988, 2002; Craske 1999). By definition, a panic attack is a sudden onset of intense fear, terror, or dread often associated with feelings of impending doom. Panic attacks, particularly a person's first panic attack, seem to occur out of the blue. Some people even have panic attacks in their sleep.

A panic attack is an abrupt surge of intense emotion that can include a racing or pounding heart, or one that skips beats; tightness, pressure, or discomfort in your chest; a lump in your throat or choking sensation;

shortness of breath or erratic breathing; light-headedness or dizziness; tingly, prickly sensations or numbness in parts of your body; shakiness or trembling; increased sweating; nausea or butterflies; hot flashes or chills; and thoughts that you're sick, dying, or going crazy. You might think that you'll throw up, suffocate, or have a heart attack. Things might seem unreal, or you might feel detached from your body. You could feel as if you need to escape or flee the situation, or fear that you might lose control and embarrass yourself in front of others. Afterward, you might become anxious about having another panic attack and feel that you have to be on guard in case it occurs. You might avoid places or situations for fear they'll trigger a panic attack. This kind of anxiety can occur anytime you feel that something is potentially dangerous or out of your control.

The sensations associated with panic attacks would be perfectly normal and a natural bodily response to a clearly dangerous event (such as being mugged). What makes a panic attack abnormal is that it occurs unexpectedly and groundlessly, when there's no reason to be emotional or afraid (Barlow, Brown, and Craske 1994). In short, a panic attack is the right reaction at the wrong time.

Have you ever experienced a panic attack? _____

If so, did it occur unexpectedly, seemingly out of the blue? _____

What did you think was happening? _____

STRESS AND PANIC

Panic attacks often occur unexpectedly, when people feel uptight or under a great deal of stress. If someone close to you has died, if you're under considerable pressure at work or at home, or if you're having difficulties in your marriage or with your children, then you're more likely to have panic attacks if you're susceptible to panic reactions. Some people don't have panic attacks when they're emotional or under stress. Rather, they experience other types of symptoms, such as headaches, high blood pressure, or ulcers. However, if you're susceptible to experiencing panic, then even happy occasions, such as an upcoming marriage, might trigger panic attacks if they involve major changes in your life.

Stress Can Trigger a Panic Attack Even When There's No Emergency

Why do you experience panic and anxiety if you're not frightened to begin with? This is where stress is involved. Stress results in the production of chemicals (hormones) in your body that can produce anxiety symptoms. This is your body's way of staying alert and preparing to deal with the stress. Indeed, stress alone can trigger an emergency (fight or flight) response, especially in people with particular genetic, personality, and experiential vulnerabilities to respond negatively to stress. Researchers such as Mark Bouton, Susan Mineka, and David Barlow (2001) have identified the following vulnerabilities (risk factors) for experiencing panic:

✦ If your parents or other family members seemed susceptible to the negative effects of stress, then you may be predisposed to panic due to genetic influences.

✦ Temperamental or personality traits, such as a general tendency to worry or a specific fear of anxiety sensations (anxiety sensitivity), may increase your risk for experiencing panic.

✦ Early experiences with uncontrollable events such as death, divorce, out-of-control parents due to drinking or anger, and childhood exposure to chronic illnesses in the home have all been associated with an increased risk for panic.

✦ Finally, some researchers think that early emotional trauma may trigger elevated levels of stress hormones that the body then maintains through adulthood, providing "kindling" for future stress responses.

In short, feeling stressed and experiencing the chemical reactions of stress can set off the emergency response even when there's no emergency. This is particularly true if you're somehow vulnerable to stress in this way.

The Anxiety Cycle

Panic attacks are the culmination of a sequence of events (Conrod 2000). According to Conrod, and reproduced here by permission of the author, the anxiety cycle evolves in the following way:

1. **Unexpected physical sensations.** First, you experience a set of unexpected physical sensations similar to a natural emergency response produced by the body.

2. **Feeling frightened.** Second, you become frightened. The emergency response causes the brain to search for danger. When an obvious external danger can't be found, the mind looks inward and creates a reason (such as, "I'm dying" or "I'm losing control"). You fear the actual physical sensations of the emergency response. If thoughts of illness or heart attacks are in the back of your mind anyway, it's understandable that you would focus on this danger.

3. **Additional anxiety.** Such thoughts lead to additional anxiety, which then leads to further buildup of the emergency response and physical symptoms.

4. **Repetitions.** After a number of repetitions of the panic experience, the anxiety and fear can occur in response to the initial physical sensations without any conscious thoughts of danger.

WHAT IS ANXIETY SENSITIVITY?

Steven Reiss and Richard McNally were the first to propose a link between anxiety sensitivity and panic attacks in 1985. According to Reiss and McNally, anxiety sensitivity is a cognitive style that involves an extreme fear of your own anxiety symptoms. People who are highly sensitive to anxiety symptoms tend to believe that anxiety symptoms have harmful or catastrophic consequences, such as physical and mental illness, loss of control, and social embarrassment. Just as people differ in how often they have anxiety symptoms, they may also differ in how much they fear these symptoms (Reiss and McNally 1985).

Research shows that it's the fear of anxiety that makes a person susceptible to more frequent and more severe panic attacks (Taylor 1999). In fact, high AS places you at greater risk for several types of problems, such as phobias, panic attacks, substance abuse, depression, and chronic pain, depending on your strategies for coping with your fear of anxiety symptoms and your particular life experiences and circumstances. Moreover, research shows that people with high levels of AS, like Isabel at the beginning of the chapter, tend to avoid physical activity (such as exercise, sex, or stair climbing), because it produces some of the same physiological sensations associated with anxiety (McWilliams and Asmundson 2001). Avoiding physical activity not only serves to maintain fear of the sensations but also cuts you off from an effective strategy for coping with anxiety and depression.

TYPES OF CONCERNS RELATED TO ANXIETY SENSITIVITY

Researchers, such as Richard Zinbarg, Timothy Brown, and David Barlow (1997), have identified three underlying dimensions or types of concerns associated with anxiety sensitivity:

1. **Physical symptoms.** Some people are more concerned about the physical symptoms of AS, due to beliefs that these sensations are signs of physical illness. For example, a person might be frightened by shortness of breath, thinking that it may result in suffocation or fainting.

2. **Psychological symptoms.** Other people are more apt to fear cognitive symptoms of AS, believing that anxiety sensations like *derealization* (feeling spaced out or detached from your immediate surroundings) are signs of mental illness. For example, some people are especially frightened by the inability to keep their minds on task because they fear going crazy.

3. **Social concerns.** Still others may fear publicly observable symptoms due to beliefs that displaying anxiety will lead to embar-

rassment, public ridicule, and social censure. These people would be embarrassed if others noticed their anxiety or nervousness.

Research on these three dimensions has enhanced our understanding of the relationship between anxiety sensitivity and various forms of anxiety-related disorders. For example, fear of physical sensations is most strongly associated with a diagnosis of panic disorder, as we saw in the case of Isabel. The fear of cognitive symptoms is more apt to be associated with depression, whereas social concerns are most strongly related to the fear of negative evaluation and to a diagnosis of social phobia, or *social anxiety disorder* (Zinbarg, Barlow, and Brown 1997).

GENDER DIFFERENCES IN ANXIETY SENSITIVITY

Studies show that men and women tend to differ when it comes to anxiety sensitivity. Women tend to show higher levels of overall AS than men, and report more physical concerns than men. Men, on the other hand, tend to report more social and psychological concerns than physical concerns related to AS (Stewart, Taylor, and Baker 1997). One study, designed to tap people's automatic associations in memory (known as the Stroop task), found that highly anxiety-sensitive women were more likely to selectively process cue words pertaining to feared physical consequences of anxiety symptoms, such as "coronary" and "suffocated," while highly anxiety-sensitive men were more apt to selectively process cue words pertaining to feared social and psychological consequences of anxiety symptoms, such as "embarrass" and "crazy" (Stewart et al. 1998). The finding that females are more fearful of the physical consequences of anxiety-related sensations than males has been found with child and adolescent samples, as well as adult samples, and could be related to gender-specific learning histories and sex-role socialization practices. Learning factors in acquiring and perpetuating anxiety sensitivity will be covered in the next chapter.

CULTURAL DIFFERENCES IN ANXIETY SENSITIVITY

Culture is presumed to shape the concerns of anxious patients (Hinton, Um, and Ba 2001). It follows that the catastrophic concerns linked to anxiety sensitivity may differ across different cultural groups. Research shows that the fear of fear can manifest in slightly different ways across different cultural groups. For some cultural groups, physical sensations, particularly heart and respiratory (wind) related symptoms, seem to cause people the most concern (Hinton et al. 2006). For other cultural groups, psychological concerns related to control are more prominent (Ramsawh 2006). Studies have found that Latin American children and adolescents express more fear of anxiety-related sensations than their white non-Latino counterparts (Weems et al. 2002b; Pina and Silverman 2004). Interestingly, because fear of anxiety-related phenomena, and physiological symptoms of anxiety in particular, may be more normative in Latino culture, there is some evidence that high AS in Latin American youth does not amplify somatic complaints in the same way as it does for white non-Latino youth (Varela et al. 2007).

CHAPTER SUMMARY

First there's fear, and then there's fear of fear. Fear is our response to an immediate threat (bear in the woods); anxiety is our anticipation of a threat (we worry that we'll meet a bear in the woods); and anxiety sensitivity is our fear of the sensations we experience when we're fearful or anxious. High levels of AS increase a person's risk for panic and other anxiety disorders. Women tend to have more physical concerns related to AS than men. Men tend to report more psychological and social concerns than physical concerns. Research shows that fears of anxiety-related sensations can vary across cultural groups.

Chapter 2

Where Does Anxiety Sensitivity Come From?

This chapter will focus on how fear of fear develops. Some evidence suggests that we inherit the tendency to be highly sensitive to anxiety-related sensations. Other evidence suggests that we learn to be especially sensitive to anxiety. Understanding the origins of a risk factor like high AS carries implications, not only for those with high AS but also for their children and other family members. For example, understanding the origins of AS may help explain why we're prone to panic attacks, why we get anxious about social situations, or why we turn to cigarettes in times of stress.

HOW DOES HIGH ANXIETY SENSITIVITY DEVELOP?

It has been over twenty years since Steven Reiss and Richard McNally proposed the idea of AS to explain why people react to anxiety in different ways. Nevertheless, we have just begun to learn about the origins of AS. Reiss and McNally believed that it could be acquired through learning, influenced by genetic factors, or both (Reiss and McNally 1985). We know that panic disorder tends to run in families, but it's not clear exactly what is passed down from one generation to the next. As researchers came to appreciate the role of AS as a risk factor for anxiety disorders, the question arose as to whether AS might explain the transmission of panic disorder.

The Role of Genetics in Anxiety Sensitivity

In 1999, Murray Stein, Kerry Jang, and John Livesley conducted the first study to examine the *heritability* of anxiety sensitivity. Heritability refers to the proportion of a characteristic that can be explained by genes. For example, if you read that shyness has a heritability factor of .40, it would mean that, on average, about 40 percent of the individual differences or variations observed in shyness may be attributable to genetics. To study heritability, researchers like to look at the differences between identical twins (twins who share *identical* DNA, the genetic blueprint for development) and fraternal twins (twins who share 50 percent of the same DNA, the same amount of DNA that sisters or brothers share, which is why these twins are called *fraternal* twins). If the levels of a certain characteristic are found to correspond more closely in identical twins than in fraternal twins, then that characteristic is presumed to have a certain measure of heritability. The greater the correspondence between identical twin pairs, the greater the heritability of that characteristic. For their study, Stein and his colleagues measured AS in 179 identical and 158 fraternal twin pairs. Results showed a greater correspondence between AS levels in identical twins than in fraternal twins. The strength of the correspondence suggested that about half of the variation in AS levels could be explained by genetic factors. When these researchers examined the data more closely, they found that AS appeared to be heritable in women but not in men. This finding may explain the increased rates of panic disorder in women as compared with men.

Finding that genes have a role to play in development of AS was exciting, but because genes accounted for only half of the variance in AS, environmental factors appeared to play an important role as well. Learning is one important environmental factor that influences many personality characteristics. That's what we'll look at now.

The Role of Learning in Anxiety Sensitivity

When adults get frightened, it's contagious, and children catch it too.

—Anonymous

Our behavior in adulthood is largely shaped by what we learned in childhood and adolescence. According to learning theory, most behavior is acquired in one of three ways:

1. Classical conditioning

2. Operant conditioning (also known as instrumental learning)

3. Vicarious conditioning

Classical conditioning is the type of learning made famous by Russian scientist Ivan Pavlov (1927) and his experiments with dogs. Pavlov was interested in the digestive system of dogs and what triggered the salivation response. First, he presented dogs with food and measured how much they drooled. Then he began ringing a bell just before presenting the food. At first, the dogs did not begin drooling until the food was presented, but after a while, the dogs began to salivate when they heard the sound of the bell. Pavlov concluded that the dogs had *learned* to associate the sound of the bell with the presentation of the food. This type of learning actually is quite common. Indeed, if you have cats, you may have noticed that they come running when you take out the can opener, even if you're opening a can of beans. The cats have *learned* to associate the sound of the can opener with their food.

This type of learning is called *classical conditioning*. Classical conditioning has been implicated in the formation of many specific fears. In 1920, John B. Watson and Rosalie Rayner conducted an experiment with an eleven-month-old baby, Little Albert, to see how emotions are learned. Watson presented a white rat and a loud noise to Little Albert. After several pairings, Albert showed fear of the white rat. It's possible that AS might develop through classical conditioning. For example, if symptoms such as dizziness or heart palpitations are paired with some inherently frightening event, such as an unexpected panic attack from out of the blue, then a person might learn to fear those symptoms in the future (Forsyth, Eifert, and Thompson 1996). However, in a study of 425 college students, Christopher Donnell and Richard McNally (1990) found that two-thirds of the students with high anxiety sensitivity had never experienced a panic attack. This suggests that classical conditioning cannot be the sole explanation for development of AS.

Take a moment to think back to when you were a child and had such symptoms as a racing heart, dizziness, shortness of breath, or strong nausea. Answer the following questions:

Did you begin to panic? _____

Did you feel weak and light-headed? _____

Did you feel as if you needed to lie down or fall down? _____

Did something frightening happen as a result of these symptoms? _____

Whereas classical conditioning is based on learning an association between two events (such as the bell and food in Pavlov's experiments with the dogs), *operant conditioning* is based on learning an association between a behavior and a consequence. Psychologist B. F. Skinner (1938), who developed the concept of operant conditioning, was influenced by the experiments of both Ivan Pavlov and John Watson. Skinner thought that the consequences of the behavior—and their impact on future behavior—were more important than the stimulus that brought on the actions. Skinner concluded that if the consequences of behavior are positive, then the behavior will more likely be repeated. On the other hand, if the consequences of behavior are negative, it's less likely to be repeated and more likely to eventually stop.

Operant conditioning is also known as *instrumental learning*, because the person's behavior is instrumental in getting something he or she wants (positive reinforcement or a reward) or removing something he or she does not want (negative reinforcement). Reinforcement, either positive or negative, increases the probability that the behavior will occur in the future. In contrast, punishment decreases the probability that a behavior will occur again in the future. Positive punishment occurs when a behavior is followed by an unpleasant consequence, such as a shock or a loud noise. Negative punishment occurs when a behavior is followed by the removal of a favorable consequence, such as taking away a child's toy after misbehavior.

Operant conditioning might contribute to development of AS if, as a child, your anxiety symptoms were rewarded in some way, such as being given special attention or positive reinforcement. Operant conditioning might also be at play in the origins of AS if you received some special dispensation as a child because of your anxiety, such as being allowed to miss school because of your anxiety symptoms. On the other hand, if your parents showed disapproval when you complained about your anxiety symptoms or they didn't listen to your complaints, the symptoms would be less likely to be displayed in the future. Research has found that positive reinforcement is the most powerful of these consequences in shaping behavior, followed by negative reinforcement and negative punishment (Mazur 2002). Positive punishment, on the other hand, such as yelling at a child to stop crying, may be effective in reducing behavior in the short term but may not be effective in modifying behavior in the long term. In fact, positive punishment may make things worse by invoking other negative responses, such as anger and resentment.

Reflect again upon when you had such symptoms as a racing heart, dizziness, shortness of breath, or strong nausea. What did your parents do when you experienced these symptoms? How did they respond to your symptoms?

Did they encourage you to stay home from school? _____

Did you receive special care? For example, did your parents sit with you or give you special foods or presents? _____

Did your parents warn you of the possible dangers of your symptoms?
_____

Did they give you medication? _____

Did they insist you go to your family doctor? _____

A third type of learning is called *observational learning* or *vicarious conditioning*. This type of learning involves learning by watching others (Bandura 1986). Albert Bandura did not believe that learning was dependent on the child's being directly rewarded or reinforced for his or her behavior. He proposed that sometimes learning occurs by observing the consequences of the behavior of role models (like parents). For example, if, as a child, you witnessed your parents exhibiting fear of anxiety symptoms and other people reinforcing their complaints about the fear by giving them more attention and care, then you might be more apt to exhibit fear of these symptoms in adulthood.

Think back again to when you were a child. Do you recall your parents displaying such symptoms as a racing heart, dizziness, shortness of breath, or strong nausea? Do you remember how they reacted to their own symptoms?

Did they stay home from work or cut back on household chores?
_____

Did they cut back on social activities? _____

Did they seem to worry about their symptoms? _____

Did they take medication? _____

Did other people seem sympathetic to their symptoms? _____

Indirect learning could also happen if your parents verbally transmitted their fears of anxiety symptoms by warning you of the harmfulness of such symptoms. Support for the role of operant conditioning in AS development comes from a study by Christopher Donnell and Richard McNally in 1990, who found that a family history of panic was associated with high AS levels in a sample of university students. The authors suggested that high AS may result from children's exposure to parental models who displayed fear of their own anxiety experiences. Of course, it could be argued that finding a familial link between AS and panic is just further evidence for the role of genetics.

In one of our own studies, we found that both operant and observational learning contribute to AS development (Watt, Stewart, and Cox

1998). We found that AS levels in early adulthood corresponded to the participants' reports of their experiences in childhood. Young adults with high AS reported more instances in which they were rewarded by parents for exhibiting anxiety symptoms in childhood as compared with controls. These young adults with high AS also reported more instances in which their parents modeled fear reactions to anxiety symptoms or verbally communicated their beliefs about the harmfulness of such symptoms. For example, their parents may have appeared frightened by the symptoms and warned them that such symptoms could quickly get worse and run out of control. These findings were replicated in two subsequent studies (Stewart et al. 2001; Watt and Stewart 2000).

The Role of Attachment in Anxiety Sensitivity

Another important learning experience derives from our early experience of forming attachment relationships with others. According to attachment theory (Bowlby 1988), the way our primary caregivers (typically parents) respond to our needs early in life establishes our enduring expectancies regarding how others will respond to us when we're in distress. For example, if your parents provided consistent and responsive care, you'd likely develop a secure attachment style. In other words, you'd develop an internal model of yourself as being valued and self-sufficient, as well as a model of others as being caring and trustworthy. If your parents were inconsistently responsive or rejecting, however, you might've developed an insecure attachment style, which means that you'd develop negative internalized models of yourself and others.

Our model of self may range from no anxiety about rejection or abandonment to intense anxiety about rejection based on beliefs of personal unworthiness. Our model of others could range from interpersonal trust to mistrust, avoidance of others, and discomfort with interpersonal closeness. Researchers generally agree that there are four possible attachment styles: *secure* (positive self and positive others), *preoccupied* (negative self and positive others), *fearful* (negative self and negative others), and *dismissing* (positive self and negative others). Although secure attachment is considered to be a protective factor, insecure attachment has been found to be associated with psychopathology (Mickelson, Kessler, and Shaver 1997; Rutter 1997). Wendy Silverman and Carl Weems (1999) first raised the possibility that insecurely attached individuals could be predisposed to misinterpret benign symptoms of anxiety as catastrophic (high AS). Carl Weems, Steven L. Berman, and other researchers (2002a) tested this hypothesis that insecurely attached individuals have higher levels of AS with a sample of high-school students and a sample of undergraduate students. They found that those who were classified as preoccupied and fearful revealed significantly higher levels of AS than those with secure and dismissing attachment styles. One of the authors (Margo Watt), along with Lachlan McWilliams and Anna Campbell (2005), conducted a study that successfully replicated and extended the 2002 findings of Weems and his research partners'. We found that attachment insecurity in both romantic and nonromantic relationships, particularly insecurity characterized by a negative model of self (fearful and preoccupied), was associated with elevated levels of AS. The model of others played a more limited role in relation to AS.

In another investigation of the origins of AS, Christine Scher and Murray Stein (2003) examined the degree to which rejection and hostile, threatening, or aggressive behavior by parents affected the severity of anxiety symptoms in young adults. In this study, Scher and Stein explored the role of childhood exposure to parental threatening, hostile, and rejecting behavior in AS development. They found that the degree of childhood exposure to these three types of parental behaviors predicted levels of AS in a sample of young adults. Even more interesting was that different types of parental behaviors predicted different types of concerns related to AS. For example, threatening behavior in the parent predicted social concerns related to AS for the young adult, whereas hostile and rejecting behavior of the parent predicted psychological concerns related to AS, such as loss of control or mental illness.

Research suggests that not only do the learning experiences of men and women differ, but these different learning experiences may also explain the different manifestations of AS in men and women. As discussed in the previous chapter, men tend to report more social concerns (fear of public embarrassment) and psychological concerns (fear of insanity or losing control) than physical concerns related to anxiety sensitivity. Women, in turn, tend to report more physical concerns (fear of death or illness) than either social or psychological concerns. The finding that women are more apt to fear potentially harmful physical consequences of anxiety symptoms is consistent with gender differences in the relative focus of common fears (Stewart, Taylor, and Baker 1997). It's possible that women may have experienced greater rewards in their learning histories for expressing body-focused complaints than men. This might explain why women have a higher frequency of medically unexplained physical complaints and worries about physical illness.

According to the American Psychiatric Association (APA 2000), worry about physical illness may represent a culturally shaped "idiom of distress" that people learn to employ in order to express concerns about more general personal and social problems. In other words, talking about physical symptoms may be a more socially acceptable way of expressing distress in some cultures. If this "idiom of distress" is more encouraged among women than men in our culture, then women who fear anxiety may come to focus on anticipated physical consequences (illness or death) when experiencing anxiety symptoms, consistent with their gender-specific learning histories. In contrast, males learn at an early age that it's less acceptable for them to lose control or display their anxiety publicly (Bronson 1966). This might explain why males who fear their anxiety symptoms may be concerned about breaking established social conventions about how men are supposed to behave, and spend more time than women worrying about losing control or acting in an embarrassing manner as a result of their anxiety.

While each child is born with his or her own distinct genetic potential for physical, social, emotional, and cognitive development, the possibilities for reaching that potential remain tied to early life experiences and the parent-child relationship within the family.

—Bernice Weissbourd

So it seems that the origins of anxiety sensitivity appear to lie partly in our genes and partly in our environment. Indeed, it's likely that genetic and learning factors interact, although this has not been investigated yet. For example, parents may respond more to a child with an inherited propensity to fear bodily sensations, and vicarious and instrumental learning factors may serve to activate or intensify inherited susceptibilities toward AS. We cannot change our genes or our learning histories; neither can we avoid anxiety. What we can do, however, is *learn* new ways of thinking and behaving when confronted with anxiety, which is the focus of this book. It's also worth noting that, whereas we can't change our own learning histories, we can influence (though not entirely control) the learning histories of our children. The skills you'll learn in this book can benefit your children as much as yourself.

CHAPTER SUMMARY

There's evidence that genes play a role in anxiety-sensitivity development, especially in women. Life experience also plays a role; in particular, if your parents responded to your anxiety symptoms and complaints, such as allowing you to miss school or skip a play rehearsal because you were too anxious, you're at greater risk for developing high AS. We still don't know how genetic and learning factors interact, but hopefully, further research will be conducted in this area.

Chapter 3

How Do You Know if You Have High Anxiety Sensitivity?

At this point in the book, you may wonder whether you have high anxiety sensitivity. Indeed, you may have recognized some of the signs of high AS when you picked up the book in the first place. In any event, this chapter will help you assess your level of sensitivity to anxiety-related sensations. We'll review the signs of AS and examine some vignettes of people with high AS. Later in the chapter, you'll find some questions that may help you determine whether this book is intended for you. Finally, we'll look at why it's important to know whether you have high anxiety sensitivity.

Nothing in life is to be feared. It is only to be understood.

—Marie Curie

As previously discussed, we all know what it feels like to have anxiety, but the way we respond to anxiety may vary. For example, most of us experience some apprehension about speaking in public. Preparing to make a speech may bring on sensations of anxiety, such as a pounding heart, rapid breathing, shaking, sweating, nausea, and feeling spacey or "zoned out." Most of us notice these sensations but expect that they'll diminish once we start talking and disappear when we finish. Some of us, however, are inclined to misinterpret these sensations, believing that they signify harmful consequences, such as a heart attack, asthma attack, or other illness; fainting; or going crazy. Some of us are inclined to fear the fear, that is, some of us have *high anxiety sensitivity*.

DETERMINING WHETHER YOU HAVE HIGH ANXIETY SENSITIVITY

As you've learned in this book, fear of fear, or high anxiety sensitivity, is the tendency to misinterpret the sensations that accompany anxiety. If you're highly sensitive to anxiety sensations, then you're apt to pay close attention to these sensations when they occur. Paying close attention to them is like amplifying, or "turning up the volume" on, the sensations. Amplification leads to a heightened state of anxiety and sometimes can lead to a panic attack. If you're not particularly sensitive to anxiety, however, you'll notice the sensations but assume that they're harmless and will pass; you'll redirect your attention elsewhere. In effect, you'll "turn down the volume" on the sensations.

People who are highly sensitive to anxiety sensations have a lower tolerance for anxiety-provoking situations than people who are less sensitive to these sensations. As a result, people with high AS tend to avoid situations that induce such feelings. These situations could include physical activities such as running, climbing stairs, or having sex; drinking caffeine; or stressful situations like speaking in public (McWilliams and Asmundson 2001). For people with high AS, their fear of fear may limit their range of activities. Again, while this fear might result in some minor health benefits, such as reducing caffeine consumption, limiting participation in physical activities may lead to other problems (such as obesity).

Case Vignette: Jacob

Jacob is a forty-year-old man who fears crossing bridges. Recent news accounts about collapsing bridges and overpasses have only served to heighten his concern. One day, Jacob drives across a bridge on his way to work. It's a blustery day, and he feels the bridge swaying in the wind. Jacob starts thinking that the bridge might collapse. His heart starts racing, he begins to feel shortness of breath, and he feels dizzy and disoriented. He begins to wonder if he's having a heart attack or perhaps going crazy; his panic mounts. Indeed, Jacob becomes anxious about being anxious and, in turn, his fear of bridges becomes amplified. He may even start avoiding using the bridge out of fear of experiencing those same sensations. Jacob has high anxiety sensitivity.

Case Vignette: Solène

Solène is a fourteen-year-old girl who doesn't like taking part in her physical education class. Indeed, she will go to great lengths to avoid participating in class activities, including purposely forgetting to bring her gym clothes. It's not that Solène doesn't like her teacher or her classmates, but she dislikes the feelings she experiences during physical activity, especially when she's running. As her heart rate and respiration increase, so does the sense of dread that something awful will happen; she fears that these sensations mean that she'll faint or fall down. She can imagine the embarrassment and humiliation she would suffer if she fainted or fell. Solène has high anxiety sensitivity. In Solène's case, she's caught in a vicious cycle in which her fear of fear amplifies her fear of exercise, and her avoidance of exercise serves to reinforce her fears.

Case Vignette: Emelyne

Emelyne is a twenty-one-year-old woman who has played the piano for a number of years. She plays for pleasure but has never enjoyed performing for others. Her fear of being criticized makes her very anxious in social situations. Nonetheless, Emelyne's friends have convinced her to enter a talent competition being held at her university. With mounting apprehension, she waits to go onstage for her recital. Her stomach is in knots, her head is pounding, and she fears she might be ill. She worries that she'll be so nervous that her wobbly legs will lead her to trip as she approaches the piano. Emelyne has high anxiety sensitivity. If she decides not to perform because of her anxiety symptoms, it may be a long time before she performs in public again.

Do any of these scenarios sound familiar to you? If so, you might have high anxiety sensitivity. To determine if someone has high anxiety sensitivity, researchers and clinicians use questionnaires and behavioral measures, such as measuring a person's response to a respiratory challenge by having him or her breathe through a straw. Research by Wendy Holloway and Richard McNally (1987) and others, such as Ronald Rapee (1994), has shown that people with high AS but no history of panic attacks respond to these respiratory challenges just as do people with panic disorder. For example, when high-AS people in Holloway and McNally's study were instructed to breathe rapidly (thirty breaths per minute) for five minutes, they reported more frequent and more intense hyperventilation sensations and a higher level of subjective anxiety than did low-AS people. The magnitude of the increased reactivity to hyperventilation sensations remained greater in the high-AS group than in the low-AS group. These findings resemble those obtained when panic patients perform tests that mimic the sensation of hyperventilation or other anxiety-inducing situations.

The most commonly used measure of hypersensitivity to anxiety sensations is the Anxiety Sensitivity Index (ASI; 1987), which was developed by Steven Reiss, Rolf Peterson, David Gursky, and Richard McNally. The ASI is a brief, sixteen-item self-report questionnaire that asks respondents to indicate how much each item applies to them on a scale of 0 (very little) to 4 (very much). The ASI assesses for the three types of concerns associated with anxiety sensitivity: physical concerns (such as the fear that nausea signifies impending physical illness), psychological concerns (such as the fear that a sense of unreality means mental illness), and social concerns (such as the fear that shakiness will be ridiculed by others).

The sixteen-item ASI is reproduced here. Read the statements carefully and consider how relevant each is to your own experience with anxiety. For example, consider how often you think this way. Respond to each item by circling one of the five corresponding numbers using the following answer key: 0 = very little, 1 = a little, 2 = some, 3 = much, and 4 = very much. Circle the number that best represents the extent to which you agree with the item. If any of the items concerns something that is not part of your experience (for example, "It scares me when I feel shaky" for someone who has never trembled or had the "shakes"), answer on the basis of how you expect to, or think you might, feel if you had such an experience. Otherwise, answer all items on the basis of your own experience.

Anxiety Sensitivity Index (ASI)

1. It is important to me not to appear nervous.   0 1 2 3 4

2. I cannot keep my mind on a task; I worry that I might be going crazy.   0 1 2 3 4

3. It scares me when I feel "shaky" (tremble).   0 1 2 3 4

4. It scares me when I feel faint.   0 1 2 3 4

5. It is important to me to stay in control of my emotions.   0 1 2 3 4

6. It scares me when my heart beats rapidly.   0 1 2 3 4

7. It embarrasses me when my stomach growls.   0 1 2 3 4

8. It scares me when I am nauseous.   0 1 2 3 4

9. When I notice that my heart is beating rapidly, I worry that I might have a heart attack.   0 1 2 3 4

10. It scares me when I become short of breath.   0 1 2 3 4

11. When my stomach is upset, I worry that I might be seriously ill.   0 1 2 3 4

12. It scares me when I am unable to keep my mind on a task.   0 1 2 3 4

13. Other people notice when I feel shaky.   0 1 2 3 4

14. Unusual body sensations scare me.   0 1 2 3 4

15. When I am nervous, I worry that I might be mentally ill.   0 1 2 3 4

16. It scares me when I am nervous.   0 1 2 3 4

There is no specific cut-off score which indicates high AS. Studies with normative samples tend to find that people score between 14 and 22. Recent studies conducted by Brad Schmidt and colleagues (2005), and others (such as Bernstein et al. 2006) suggest that ASI scores exceeding 30 indicate high AS levels.

Why is it important to assess our sensitivity to anxiety sensations? Because the first step in change is awareness. Recognizing our fear of fear allows us to begin the process of reducing our AS and its negative impact on our lives. Reducing our fear of fear will reduce our risk for debilitating anxiety disorders associated with high AS. These disorders may include panic disorder (persistent occurrence and fear of panic attacks) and social phobia (intense fear of being judged negatively in social situations). Reducing levels of AS may reduce a person's risk for disorders related to anxiety, such as hypochondriasis (fear of illness), chronic pain, or substance abuse. Reducing levels of AS can confer both immediate and long-term benefits. For example, reducing our fear of fear may open up options for more fun and socializing if we stop avoiding social activities. Reducing our fear of fear means we'll be less apt to end up in emergency rooms for assessments of nonexistent heart attacks or fictional brain tumors. Such experiences can actually fuel concerns about our health. Reducing our fear of fear can enhance our physical well-being if we become more physically active and reduce our risk for the harmful effects of inactivity (such as obesity, type 2 diabetes, and cardiovascular ailments). Reducing our fear of fear means that we'll be less apt to avoid feared situations, people, and tasks, and more apt to approach opportunities for actualizing our potential, being the best we can be.

CHAPTER SUMMARY

People with fear of fear are highly sensitive to the sensations associated with anxiety and tend to pay close attention to these sensations when they arise. This increased attention amplifies the sensations, leading to a heightened state of anxiety and, potentially, a panic attack. Amplification of sensations can lead to avoidance behavior, which only serves to maintain the fear. Knowing that you're prone to amplify anxiety-related sensations—in other words, highly anxiety sensitive—is the first step to understanding how to reduce fear of fear. You may be someone who fears the physical consequences of anxiety (you fear illness when your breathing is compromised) or anxiety sensations (you fear losing control when you can't think straight), or fears the social consequences (you fear embarrassment when your voice shakes). Whatever the case, learning to reduce your fear of fear can lead to a greater comfort level in social situations, fewer concerns about health, reduced need for cigarettes or alcohol to cope with tension and stress, and perhaps increased participation in physical activity. Reducing your fear of fear could change your life if it leads you to avail yourself of more opportunities to make friends, take on challenges, explore new options, and realize personal growth and fulfillment.

Part II

Why Is Anxiety Sensitivity Important?

Chapter 4

Anxiety Sensitivity as a Risk Factor for Anxiety Disorders

Worry gives a small thing a big shadow.

—Swedish proverb

In this chapter, we'll look at the role of anxiety sensitivity in various anxiety disorders. Because AS amplifies anxiety responses (as mentioned in chapter 3), it can contribute to the development of panic symptoms. Indeed, research shows that AS is high in people suffering from panic disorder (Stewart, Knize, and Pihl 1992; Taylor, Koch, and McNally 1992). Studies tracking people over time show that high-AS people are more likely than others to develop panic attacks under stressful life circumstances (Schmidt, Lerew, and Jackson 1997). Whereas a lot of research has focused on panic disorder, AS also has been linked to a number of other anxiety disorders, including social phobia (social anxiety disorder) and post-traumatic stress disorder (PTSD). We'll look at these disorders in this chapter.

PANIC DISORDER

Consider this conversation between Holly and Fred, characters in Truman Capote's novella *Breakfast at Tiffany's* (1958, 40):

Holly: "Listen, you know those days when you get the mean reds?"

Fred: "The mean reds? You mean like the blues?"

Holly: "No, the blues are because you're getting fat or because it's been raining too long. You're just sad, that's all. The mean reds are horrible. Suddenly you're afraid, and you don't know what you're afraid of. Do you ever get that feeling?"

What Is Panic Disorder?

The "mean reds" to which Holly refers sound like panic symptoms. Panic symptoms were first described by Hippocrates around 400 BCE. The term "panic" comes from the Greek god Pan, who was said to take pleasure in frightening (panicking) people and animals in the woods (Barlow 1988). Apparently, a sudden shout from Pan was sufficient to put them to flight (Graves 1960). Pan could make his appearance (attack) *unexpectedly*, thus satisfying an important definitional feature of the panic attacks experienced by people with panic disorder (Ley 1992).

According to the American Psychiatric Association (APA 2000), a panic attack is a discrete period of intense fear or discomfort. Four (or more) of the following symptoms develop abruptly and reach a peak within ten minutes:

- ✦ palpitations, pounding heart, or accelerated heart rate

- ✦ sweating

- ✦ trembling or shaking

- ✦ sensations of shortness of breath or smothering

- ✦ feeling of choking

- ✦ chest pain or discomfort

- ✦ nausea or abdominal distress

- ✦ feeling dizzy, unsteady, light-headed, or faint

+ derealization (feelings of unreality) or depersonalization (being detached from oneself)

+ fear of losing control or going crazy

+ fear of dying

+ paresthesia (numbness or tingling sensations)

+ chills or hot flashes

Panic attacks are relatively common. In fact, research shows that about 25 percent of first-year college or university students report having had at least one panic attack in the previous year (Brown and Cash 1989). People who experience recurrent unexpected panic attacks may eventually develop full-blown panic disorder, especially people who experience persistent concern about having additional attacks and worry about the implications of the attack or its consequences (such as losing control, having a heart attack, or "going crazy").

Around the world, 1 to 4 percent of people suffer from full-blown panic disorder. Approximately one-third to one-half of individuals with panic disorder also have agoraphobia. *Agoraphobia* refers to significant anxiety about being in places or situations from which escape might be difficult or even embarrassing if the person had a panic attack. Agoraphobic fears typically include being outside one's home alone; being in a crowd or standing in a line; crossing a bridge; and traveling in a bus, train, or car (APA 2000).

Have you ever experienced a sudden onset of intense anxiety symptoms (racing heart, profuse sweating, or dizziness)? _____

Did the symptoms seem to arise out of the blue? _____

What kinds of situations tend to provoke your anxiety or panic? _____

Anxiety Sensitivity and Panic Disorder

High anxiety sensitivity is a known risk factor for panic disorder. In his 1999 book *Anxiety Sensitivity: Theory, Research, and Treatment of the Fear of Anxiety*, Steven Taylor reviews the links between AS and the simultaneous development of panic attacks and panic disorder. Early studies showed that levels of AS (fear of fear) distinguished people who had experienced panic attacks (but not panic disorder) from people who had never had a panic attack (Norton, Cox, and Malan 1992) and from those with confirmed panic disorder (Cox, Endler, and Swinson 1991). Consistently, patients with panic disorder are found to have higher levels of AS than all other anxiety disorder groups except post-traumatic stress disorder (PTSD) (Taylor, Koch, McNally, and Crockett 1992).

Anxiety sensitivity also has been linked to difficulties in getting off of anti-anxiety medications. For example, high AS levels are the best predictor of panic-disorder patients' lack of success in stopping benzodiazepine medication (drugs such as Valium, Librium, and Halcion). High AS levels also are associated with people's inability to abstain from medication whether or not they are also receiving psychotherapy (Bruce et al. 1995).

The most convincing evidence that people with elevated levels of AS are at risk for developing panic disorder comes from studies conducted by Norman B. Schmidt and colleagues at Florida State University. In 1997, Schmidt, Darin Lerew, and Robert Jackson conducted a study with over 1,400 young adults from the general population, whom they followed over time. Participants in the study were new cadets at the United States Air Force Academy (USAFA), who were undergoing the highly stressful five-week basic cadet training. The researchers found that cadets who scored high on the Anxiety Sensitivity Index (ASI; Peterson and Reiss 1992) were three times more likely to experience unexpected panic attacks during the five weeks of basic training than those cadets who scored low on the ASI. That was true even for those who had never had a panic attack before in their lives. Indeed, during basic training, 13 percent of the high-AS cadets in the study panicked, compared to only 2 percent of the low-AS cadets. In other words, a cadet scoring high on the ASI would be at risk for panic attacks during the stressful process of basic training. In a subsequent study conducted in 1999, the same researchers again followed a large group of 1,296 young adults who were going through military basic training. As in the previous study, AS predicted the development of spontaneous panic attacks during basic training. This held true even after the researchers accounted for a prior history of panic attacks or cadets' levels of trait anxiety (that is, their more general tendency to be an anxious person).

Many famous people have suffered from panic attacks. Norwegian artist Edvard Munch was known to have panic attacks, and his famous painting *The Scream* is thought to be his own depiction of a panic attack in progress. There's some evidence suggesting that Charles Darwin (1809–82) also may have suffered from panic disorder. Apparently, as an adult, he was plagued by ill health that impaired his functioning and severely limited his activities. Darwin's writings and biographical materials indicate that he probably suffered from an anxiety disorder. Apparently, his worst problems were recurrent nausea, gastrointestinal distress, headaches, and "a swimming head" (Campbell and Matthews 2005). When considered individually, Darwin's symptoms suggest the possibility of a variety of physical health conditions, but taken together they point toward panic disorder with agoraphobia. Thomas Barloon and Russell Noyes, Jr. (1997) have suggested that panic disorder with agoraphobia may explain Darwin's secluded lifestyle, including his difficulties in speaking before groups and his avoidance of meetings with coworkers.

SOCIAL PHOBIA (SOCIAL ANXIETY DISORDER)

The fear of being laughed at makes cowards of us all.

—Mignon McLaughlin

Studies show that about 20 percent of people report excessive fear of public speaking and performance. A much smaller percentage (about 10 percent), however, appear to experience enough impairment or distress to warrant a diagnosis of social phobia (Becker et al. 2002; Kessler et al. 1994, 2005). People with social phobia, also known as social anxiety disorder, suffer from a marked and persistent fear of one or more social or performance situations, such as those in which they are exposed to unfamiliar people or to possible scrutiny by others (APA 2000).

People with social phobia may feel like the proverbial deer caught in the headlights when they're in social situations. The socially anxious person fears that he or she will do something that brings humiliation or embarrassment. The person fears showing symptoms of anxiety (such as sweating, blushing, trembling, confusion, gastrointestinal distress, or diarrhea), thinking that others will judge him or her to be anxious, weak, "crazy," or stupid. In severe cases, these symptoms may meet the criteria for a panic attack. But unlike the situation with people with panic disorder, the panic attacks in people with social phobia don't happen unexpectedly. Rather, they happen when the person is in a social or performance situation, or when he or she anticipates going into such a situation. The feared social or performance situation is either avoided or endured with intense anxiety or dread. A diagnosis of social phobia is appropriate only if the avoidance, fear, or anxious anticipation of encountering the social or performance situation interferes significantly with the person's daily routine, occupational functioning, or social life; or if the person is markedly distressed about having the phobia (APA 2000). Social phobia is more prevalent among women, and typically begins during middle adolescence, around the age of fifteen (Stein, Torgrud, and Walker 2000; Wittchen, Stein, and Kessler 1999).

Do you tend to get anxious in social situations? _____

What kinds of anxiety symptoms do you experience in social situations?

_____

Do you think that people are judging you? _____

Do you avoid social situations because you find the anxiety sensations so aversive? _____

Do you avoid speaking or performing in public? _____

Anxiety Sensitivity and Social Phobia (Social Anxiety Disorder)

Anxiety sensitivity's role in social phobia possibly is due to the fear of being negatively evaluated when displaying observable symptoms of anxiety (Asmundson and Stein 1994; Ball et al. 1995; Cox, Borger, and Enns 1999; Norton et al. 1997). In 1992, Roberta Maller and Steven Reiss reported their findings on 151 college students to whom the Anxiety Sensitivity Index (ASI) had been administered in 1984. In 1987, these students were retested for AS and for panic-attack and anxiety-disorder history. Maller and Reiss found that ASI scores in 1984 predicted the frequency and intensity of panic attacks in 1987. Compared with those who had low 1984 ASI scores, students with high 1984 ASI scores were five times more likely to have an anxiety disorder during the period from 1984 to 1987.

In 1997, Ron Norton and colleagues found that levels of AS were the best predictor of self-reported anxiety related to performing in public (social performance anxiety) and a good predictor of anxiety related to interacting with others (social interaction anxiety). Some studies have found that people with social phobia can score as high or even higher on the ASI than people with panic disorder (Hazen, Walker, and Stein 1995). A. L. Hazen and colleagues found that, whereas panic disorder patients scored significantly higher on ASI items tapping fears of cardiorespiratory and other physical sensations (that is, physical concerns), social phobia patients scored significantly higher on three items tapping specific fears of displaying anxiety to others (that is, social concerns); for example, "It is important to me not to appear nervous," "It embarrasses me when my stomach growls," and "Other people notice when I feel shaky."

Recently, Noortje Vriends and colleagues (2007) looked at predictors of recovery from social phobia in a community-based sample of young German women. Initially, participants were assessed for characteristics consistent with a diagnosis of social phobia. Then these young women were reassessed for persistence of social anxiety symptoms eighteen months later. The researchers found that lower levels of AS at baseline (time of initial measurement) were a significant predictor of recovery from social phobia.

The case of Lawrence illustrates the many challenges people with social phobia face in their daily lives.

Case Vignette: Lawrence

Lawrence is a forty-six-year-old man who was required to take stress leave from work due to his social anxiety. He has wrestled with social anxiety all his life, but as he got older, his anxiety worsened and was accompanied by depression. Lawrence could trace his shyness back to childhood and his social anxiety to his teenage years. As a child and adolescent, he resented his mother's encouragement to socialize with his peers. As an adult, he avoided social events but, if required to attend, sought out the solace of alcohol to reduce his anxiety. It was on one of these occasions that he met his wife. The couple got married and had two children.

Lawrence worked as a machinist at a local fabrication shop. When the kids were young, Lawrence maintained a certain level of social participation by attending his kids' sporting events, although he stayed away from the other parents. His wife attended the parent-teacher conferences, picked up the orders for take-out food, and did the grocery shopping. As the kids got older, his social isolation intensified, as did his anxiety about social situations. At times when he felt obligated to attend a social event, he was very ill at ease, never knew what to say, and suffered the awkward silences with horror. He knew he made others uncomfortable and assumed they thought he was crazy.

The worst part for Lawrence was the anticipatory anxiety he felt in advance of having to do something in public. The more time he had to worry about these situations, the more anxious, fearful, and uncomfortable he felt. Eventually, Lawrence's anxiety became so severe that even going to work became extremely unpleasant. He would drive to work but would be unable to get out of the car. Anticipating the demands for conversation and social interaction triggered intense anxiety-related sensations and filled him with dread. His wife was increasingly frustrated and feared for their financial well-being.

When medications failed to resolve his problems, Lawrence was encouraged to see a psychologist. He was late for the first interview because, as he explained later, he wanted to be sure no one was in the waiting room. Not surprisingly, the assessment revealed that Lawrence had a high sensitivity to anxiety-related sensations (for example, blushing, trembling, dry mouth, and confusion) and intense foreboding about the social consequences of these sensations (for example, drawing the attention of and ridicule from others). Lawrence felt as if he were waging a battle with himself and losing. He was tired and felt defeated. Fortunately, he proved to be a good student of cognitive behavioral therapy, learning ways of modifying his thinking and behavior so that he was no longer a prisoner of his fears. Eventually, Lawrence was able to overcome his social anxiety using the same techniques you'll learn about in this book.

POST-TRAUMATIC STRESS DISORDER (PTSD)

The essential feature of PTSD is the development of characteristic symptoms following exposure to an extremely traumatic event. A traumatic event isn't just a stressful event; it's an experience that involves actual or threatened death or serious injury. The trauma also may threaten a person's *self-integrity*, or understanding of who he or she is. Such life experiences as being involved in military combat; becoming the victim of a violent personal assault, a rape, or a terrorist attack; and surviving a car accident, plane crash, or natural disaster all qualify as potentially traumatic experiences (APA 2000).

In PTSD, the individual's response to the event must involve intense fear, helplessness, or horror. The characteristic symptoms resulting from exposure to the trauma include persistent reexperiencing of the traumatic event (such as having nightmares or flashbacks), persistent avoidance of reminders of the trauma (avoiding places, people, or discussion of the event), persistent numbing of general responsiveness (experiencing a restricted range of emotions whereby the sufferer doesn't cry or laugh at things that normally would evoke such responses), and persistent symptoms of increased arousal or increased startle response (jumping at sudden sounds). For a diagnosis of PTSD, the full symptom picture must be present for more than one month. Also, the disturbance must cause clinically significant distress or impairment in social, occupational, or other important areas of functioning (APA 2000).

In North America, the proportion of people who've met the diagnostic criteria for PTSD at some point in their lives is around 8 percent. Studies of at-risk individuals such as combat veterans, victims of volcanic eruptions or criminal violence, emergency service workers, police officers, and sex-trade workers have yielded prevalence rates as high as 58 percent (APA 2000). For example, PTSD among combat veterans ranges from 22 to 31 percent (Kulka et al. 1990; Prigerson, Maciejewski, and Rosenheck 2002). Prevalence rates among women tend to be twice that of men (10 percent versus 5 percent, respectively; Kessler et al. 1995), even after controlling for frequency of exposure to traumatic events (Breslau 2002). This may be due to differences in the types of trauma to which men and women tend to be exposed. Men are more apt to be physically assaulted; women are more apt to be sexually assaulted. In one study of two thousand adult women who had personally experienced such trauma as rape, sexual molestation, robbery, and aggravated assault, rape had the most significant emotional impact. Almost 20 percent of the rape victims had attempted suicide, and 44 percent reported suicidal ideation following the rape (Kilpatrick et al. 1985). Other studies (Resnick et al. 1993) found that 32 percent of rape victims met criteria for PTSD at some point in their lives. Steven Taylor and William Koch (1995) found that 15 percent of adults who experienced severe auto accidents developed PTSD.

Have you ever experienced a traumatic event, such as a car accident, an assault, exposure to combat, or sudden death of a loved one? _____

Following this event, did you reexperience the trauma in nightmares or flashbacks? _____

Did you avoid places or people associated with the event? _____

Did you find yourself feeling numb or distant from others? _____

Did you find that you were unusually jumpy, or easily startled? _____

History of Post-Traumatic Stress Disorder

PTSD has a long history, although its name and description have changed over the years. At various points in its history, PTSD has been called "exhaustion" or "soldier's heart" (seen in soldiers following the stress of battle, such as the American Civil War), and "railway hysteria" (exhibited by people who had been in traumatic railway accidents). The term "shell shock" emerged during World War I, and "combat fatigue" in World War II. These various terms were used to describe the stress and anxiety exhibited by veterans of combat trauma (Parrish 2003). The term "post-traumatic stress disorder" emerged during the Vietnam War and was officially recognized in the third edition of the *Diagnostic and Statistical Manual of Mental Disorders* (APA 1980).

Anxiety Sensitivity and Post-Traumatic Stress Disorder

Several lines of evidence suggest that anxiety sensitivity plays an important role in PTSD (Taylor 2004). Research has found that AS levels are higher in people with PTSD than in those with any of the other anxiety disorders, with the exception of panic disorder (Taylor et al. 1992). Moreover, the severity of AS is correlated with the severity of PTSD symptoms (Fedoroff et al. 2000).

Steven Taylor (2004) suggests two possible explanations for the relationship between high AS and PTSD. According to Taylor, elevated AS may be a predisposing factor. In other words, AS may be a risk factor that predates the development of PTSD. People with high AS might have more-intense emotional reactions to traumatic stressors because of the amplifying nature of AS. This more-intense reaction might predispose them to develop full-blown PTSD more than other people experiencing the same traumatic event. A second possible reason for why elevated AS is seen among people with PTSD is that both might arise from exposure to a traumatic stressor. For example, being in a car accident may not only trigger PTSD but also cause the person to become fearful of anything that was present at the time of the accident, including arousal-related bodily sensations. High AS may then amplify PTSD symptoms. This being the case, the person would become alarmed at reexperiencing symptoms associated with the accident, believing that these symptoms signify harmful consequences. For example, the person may become alarmed by arousal symptoms (such as heart palpitations), believing them to be signs of some physical catastrophe to follow, such as a heart attack, not to mention being reminders of the original trauma (Fedoroff et al. 2000).

Studies have investigated the role of high AS in the development of PTSD following various traumatic events. These studies have focused on military combat (Jakupcak et al. 2006), car accidents (Fedoroff et al. 2000), violent assault (Zahradnik et al. 2007), sexual assault (Bonin et al. 2000), natural disasters (Hagh-Shenas et al. 2005), and even childbirth (Keogh, Ayers, and Francis 2002). High AS may help explain why people who develop PTSD may be at greater risk of developing other anxiety disorders and substance-related disorders (APA 1994). Indeed, research has shown that approximately 85 percent of people with PTSD report using alcohol. Many of these people would meet the criteria for substance abuse (Stewart 1996).

Sherry Stewart (1997) has suggested that people with PTSD drink to try to control their PTSD symptoms. One investigation with a large community-based sample of women who'd been sexually abused and were diagnosed with alcohol abuse or dependency found that the women's drinking problem followed the assault in every case (Winfield et al. 1990). Another study of patients with comorbid PTSD and alcohol abuse found that patients drank excessively just prior to bedtime, reportedly to control sleep disturbances and nightmares (LaCoursiere, Godfrey, and Ruby 1980). It's possible that high AS may increase the levels of substance use as a way of avoiding thinking about the trauma (Stewart 1997). The story of Marie-France (described next in this section) serves as a case in point.

Other types of trauma have not been researched as extensively as rape and military combat. For example, the trauma of giving birth has garnered relatively little attention. However, Edmund Keogh, Susan Ayers, and Harriet Francis (2002) conducted an interesting study in which they investigated whether a pregnant mother's prenatal levels of AS would predict her degree of PTSD symptoms following childbirth. Forty women completed a series of self-report measures, including the ASI (Peterson and Reiss 1992) prenatally. Two weeks postpartum, the same women completed another series of self-report measures of PTSD, mood, and birth experiences. Prenatal anxiety sensitivity predicted PTSD symptoms, suggesting that AS may act as an important vulnerability factor in adverse responses to childbirth. Chapter 5 examines the role of AS in labor pain and presents the case of a first-time mother with high AS, to better convey how AS may operate as a risk factor during childbirth.

Even people who provide assistance in the aftermath of a traumatic event can be susceptible to PTSD symptoms. Iranian researchers Hagh-Shenas and colleagues (2005) compared the psychological status of trained rescue personnel to that of untrained university student volunteers in responding to an earthquake. One hundred student volunteers, eighteen Red Crescent workers, and thirty-six firefighters participated in this study. One of the most significant findings of this study was that untrained volunteers revealed more symptoms of PTSD. Moreover, those helpers with higher scores on the ASI showed greater adverse psychological effects.

Case Vignette: Marie-France

Marie-France worked as a waitress and took courses part-time at the local college. She really enjoyed her American literature course, which was taught by a visiting professor from Chicago. Sometimes work demands required that she miss a class. Following one such occasion, she was alarmed by a call from her professor suggesting that they meet in person to discuss her progress in the course.

When she arrived at his office, he invited her to have a glass of wine. She accepted the drink to avoid appearing impolite, plus she welcomed its tension-reducing effects. However, she did not welcome what happened next. In retrospect, she thinks the professor must have laced her drink with Rohypnol (the date-rape drug). She recalls very little between taking the drink and becoming aware of being sexually violated. As she struggled to escape, he threatened her not to tell because no one would believe her story. Marie-France made her way to a friend's house. She told her friend but was reticent to report the assault to police or university officials, fearing the stress of a "he said, she said" scenario.

She dropped out of class. Persistent nightmares of being pursued by her assailant made sleep impossible. She was fearful about returning to work in case her assailant called or showed up. Her emotions seemed to fluctuate between feeling numb and aloof, and wanting to jump out of her skin when the telephone rang. The only thing that seemed to relieve her feelings of apprehension and agitation was alcohol. Indeed, by the time she presented for treatment, her drinking had become cause for concern among her friends and family. Fortunately for Marie-France, her psychologist implemented a treatment designed to target high AS, which was presumed to underlie both her PTSD symptoms and substance use. (The success of this approach to the treatment of comorbid anxiety and substance-use disorder is described in Watt et al. 2008).

CHAPTER SUMMARY

The evidence is clear: anxiety sensitivity is an important risk factor for developing anxiety disorders. Most of the research has examined the role of AS in acquiring and maintaining panic disorder. However, more recently, its role in other anxiety disorders, such as social phobia and PTSD, has garnered increased interest. Research shows that levels of AS are higher in those with panic disorder, social phobia, and PTSD than in all other anxiety disorders, and are significantly higher than levels found in the general community. Indeed, evidence suggests that people with elevated levels of AS are predisposed to experience panic attacks in response to stressful conditions (such as military cadet training) and PTSD symptoms in response to traumatic events (such as rape, earthquake, and even childbirth). If you have high AS and any of these comorbid conditions, you're not alone. Consider getting help from a professional. There are ways to relieve your symptoms and improve your quality of life, and a good first step is to read on.

Chapter 5

The Role of Anxiety
Sensitivity in Other Disorders

In chapter 4, we looked at the role of anxiety sensitivity in various anxiety disorders. This chapter will focus on AS's role in other anxiety-related disorders. More specifically, we'll examine the relationship between AS and depression, health anxiety (including hypochondriasis), chronic pain, substance abuse, and other problems, such as menstrual distress.

DEPRESSION

One thing the blues ain't, is funny.

—Stephen Stills

Apparently, the use of the word "blue" to mean sad dates from the late 1300s. Feeling blue, or down in the dumps, from time to time is a normal part of everyday life. Most cases of the blues disappear quickly and don't prevent us from finding enjoyment in life. On the other hand, feeling sad or depressed for extended periods can indicate that something more serious is going on. According to the American Psychiatric Association (APA 2000), to be diagnosed with major depression, a person must exhibit at least five of the following symptoms, and these must persist for at least two weeks:

- A persistently sad, anxious, or empty mood

- Loss of interest in activities previously enjoyed

- Excessive crying

- Decreased ability to concentrate and make decisions

- Decreased energy

- Thoughts of suicide or suicide attempts

- Weight gain or loss

- Social withdrawal

- Changes in sleep patterns

- Increased restlessness and irritability

- Feelings of helplessness, guilt, or hopelessness

- Physical ailments that don't respond to standard treatment (such as chronic headaches)

Approximately 1 percent of men and 2 percent of women are clinically depressed at any one point in time. And about 5 percent of men and 10 percent of women experience clinical depression at some point in their lives. *Women are at twice the risk as men* of experiencing depression, a risk that emerges in early adolescence and persists throughout adulthood. Regardless of gender, once you've had one experience of clinical depression, you have a high risk for repeated experiences of depression (Canadian Psychological Association 2006).

1. Have there been times when you felt intense sadness lasting more than a few days but not for two weeks or longer? _____

2. Have there been times when you didn't have the energy to get out of bed? _____

3. Have there been times when you withdrew from friends? _____

4. Have there been times when you found it difficult to find joy in life? _____

5. Have there been times when you contemplated self-harm (such as suicide)? _____

If you suffer from persistent feelings of low mood, irritability, disrupted sleep and appetite, withdrawal from friends, or thoughts of self-harm, you should speak to a professional, such as your family physician or mental health worker. Let someone know you're hurting.

Anxiety Sensitivity and Depression

Researchers were somewhat surprised to find a relationship between anxiety sensitivity and depression (Otto et al. 1995; Taylor et al. 1996). As Steven Taylor suggests, it's not intuitively obvious why there should be a relationship between fear of fear and depression (1999). Nonetheless, in 1995, Michael Otto, of Boston University, and his colleagues found that depressed individuals reported higher scores on the Anxiety Sensitivity Index (ASI) than nondepressed controls. Indeed, the scores of depressed individuals were as high as those of people with social phobia and generalized anxiety disorder. In the previously mentioned 1997 study of military cadets undergoing basic training (see chapter 4), cadets' scores on the ASI unexpectedly predicted their levels of depression, in addition to predicting the occurrence of panic attacks (Schmidt, Lerew, and Jackson 1997).

Since then, several studies have found that the psychological-concerns component of AS (such as the fear of losing control when anxious) is more predictive of depressive symptoms than either physical-concerns (such as fear of having a heart attack) or social-concerns (such as fear of embarrassment when appearing anxious to others) components (Cox, Enns, and Taylor 2001; Rector, Szacun-Shimizu, and Leybman 2007). Indeed, Steven Taylor refers to the fear of losing control as a "depression-specific form of anxiety sensitivity" (Taylor et al. 1996, 478). In particular, symptoms of depression (rather than anxiety) may be amplified by fear of losing control. The need to maintain control is known to be a central factor in most theories of depression (see Watt 2001). Certainly, the need to stay in control can be exhausting and, since many things in life are out of our control, sets an impossible standard. Trying to maintain control can lead to feelings of discouragement, helplessness, and eventually hopelessness.

To understand how AS can be related to depression, let's consider the case of Molly.

Case Vignette: Molly

Molly is a twenty-eight-year-old graduate student who has struggled with episodes of depression for the past ten years. Antidepressants relieve her most troubling symptoms (fatigue; irritability; and loss of appetite, sleep, and pleasure) during her worst episodes. Molly finds it difficult to identify triggers for her depression. She decides to try psychotherapy and makes an appointment with a psychologist on campus. During the assessment process, the psychologist identifies that Molly seems to be highly anxiety sensitive. Closer examination reveals that she particularly fears losing control when experiencing strong emotions, such as anxiety. As it turns out, certain aspects of graduate school are especially likely to provoke a sense of helplessness or loss of control, for example, conducting lab demonstrations and attending formal meetings with her thesis supervisor. Molly's need for control in an environment (such as graduate school) where many things can't easily be controlled makes her vulnerable. She is vulnerable to feelings of helplessness and hopelessness. In Molly, the fear of losing control triggers symptoms of depression rather than anxiety.

HEALTH ANXIETY (INCLUDING HYPOCHONDRIASIS)

He is the querulous, bedridden **valetudinarian** *complaining of his asthma or his hay fever, remarking with characteristic hyperbole that "every speck of dust suffocates me."*

—Oliver Conant, reviewing *Marcel Proust: Selected Letters Volume Two, 1904–1909*

A *valetudinarian* is a rather formal term for a person who is unduly anxious about his or her health. Today, we would describe someone with a lot of health anxiety, like Proust, as being a hypochondriac. *Health anxiety* refers to a continuum of health-related fears and beliefs ranging from no concern about bodily sensations at one end, to extreme fear of and preoccupation with bodily sensations at the other (Hadjistavropoulos, Asmundson, and Kowalyk 2004). Hypochondriasis is a severe form of health anxiety characterized by an intense fear of having a serious disease, a fear that's not relieved when a medical examination finds no evidence of disease. People with hypochondriasis can often acknowledge that their fears are unrealistic, but this doesn't reduce their anxiety. For a diagnosis of hypochondriasis, a person's preoccupation with fear of disease must cause a great deal of distress or interfere with his or her ability to perform important activities, such as work, school, or family and social responsibilities.

Marcel Proust seems to have had some insight into his extreme health anxiety, as evidenced by this quote: "For each illness that doctors cure with medicine, they provoke ten in healthy people by inoculating them with the virus that is a thousand times more powerful than any microbe: the idea that one is ill" (1925).

Do you worry about your health? _____

Do you tend to scan your body for lumps and bumps? _____

Do you visit your doctor more often than other people you know do?

_____

If you hear about a disease on TV, do you worry that you might have it?

_____

Anxiety Sensitivity and Hypochondriasis

The role of anxiety sensitivity in both acquisition and persistence of hypochondriasis has garnered some attention from researchers. In 1999, Winnipeg clinical psychologist Brian J. Cox found elevated levels of AS (relative to healthy controls) in a sample of patients with primary hypochondriasis. AS has been shown to correlate with hypochondriacal concerns in people suffering from panic disorder (Otto et al. 1992), people suffering from major depression (Otto et al. 1998), and even healthy undergraduates (Stewart and Watt 2000).

In 2000, the present authors investigated childhood learning experiences possibly associated with acquiring high hypochondriacal concerns in a sample of healthy young adults. In our study, we found that participants who reported more learning experiences related to bodily symptoms (anxiety symptoms, and aches and pains) revealed higher levels of AS and hypochondriacal concerns than study participants who did not report as many such learning experiences. These learning experiences included being rewarded in some way when they had such bodily symptoms, for example, being allowed to stay home from school. Other learning experiences included parents exhibiting more fears about such symptoms and conveying their fears to their children. In addition, we found evidence that suggested that these learning experiences led to an elevated level of anxiety sensitivity, which, in turn, led to elevated levels of hypochondriacal concerns. We concluded that elevated AS is a risk factor for acquiring hypochondriasis. Let's look at the case of Kirsten, who was seen at one of the authors' clinics:

Case Vignette: Kirsten

Kirsten was a forty-two-year-old, married mother of three daughters who worked part-time as a bank teller. She presented with a persistent fear of breast cancer and a preoccupation with the belief that she may have developed malignant breast tumors. Assessment revealed that Kirsten was highly sensitive to anxiety-related sensations, in particular, physical sensations associated with anxiety. Before the onset of Kirsten's illness, a female relative had developed breast cancer and had undergone a radical mastectomy. Kirsten herself had discovered small lumps in her breasts and had consulted her physician, fearing that she had developed breast cancer. Medical tests revealed that her physical symptoms indicated nonmalignant fibroid masses that didn't require intervention. For several months before her psychological assessment, Kirsten had visited her family physician twice a month for breast examinations. These tests temporarily allayed her fears, but worries about developing breast cancer returned within days or even hours of her visits to the physician. These concerns significantly affected her personal life and work. Intrusive thoughts about breast cancer interfered with her ability to concentrate while at her bank job. She found touching or looking at her own breasts so highly distressful that she had her husband help her put on her brassiere and apply creams or sunscreen in any area around her chest. Kirsten reported that she avoided the news and women's magazines for fear that she would come across an article or news item on breast cancer, which she found extremely distressful. She also avoided visiting the relative who'd had the mastectomy, because she found such contact upsetting.

Kirsten reported a strong fear of death, involving concerns that she would die from breast cancer and leave her three children motherless. Her husband had become exasperated with the demands she placed on him. Her family physician had also become frustrated about Kirsten's constant need for reassurance. Fortunately, her physican referred her for psychological assessment and possible cognitive behavioral therapy.

ANXIETY SENSITIVITY AND CHRONIC PAIN

The greatest evil is physical pain.

—St. Augustine

Recently, researchers have begun examining the role of anxiety sensitivity in conditions such as chronic pain (Asmundson, Wright, and Hadjistavropoulos 2005; Stewart and Asmundson 2006). The first study to actually include measures of both AS and pain was conducted in 1991 by Toronto psychiatrist Klaus Kuch and his colleagues. These researchers found that panic-disorder patients with chronic pain reported significantly higher levels of AS than panic-disorder patients without chronic pain. In a subsequent study of fifty-five auto-accident survivors with chronic pain, Kuch and colleagues (1994) found that those with accident phobia reported higher levels of AS and pain in more areas of the body.

Gordon Asmundson and Ron Norton (1995) found that chronic back-pain patients with high AS tended to report more cognitive anxiety ("I can't think straight when I'm in pain") and more fearful appraisals about pain ("Pain sensations are terrifying") than chronic back-pain patients with low AS. High-AS and low-AS individuals didn't differ in reported pain severity; however, patients with high AS were twice as likely as patients with moderate or low levels to report use of analgesic medication to relieve pain.

In 1996, Gordon Asmundson and Steven Taylor found that AS could better explain people's fear of pain than actual pain severity in a sample of chronic-pain patients. Interestingly, it was people's AS levels, as opposed to the severity of the pain experienced, that predicted how much they avoided pain (such as by avoiding physical activity). Subsequently, Asmundson and colleagues (1999) extended these findings to a sample of patients (85 percent women) with recurring headaches. Headache patients with high AS reported more fear of pain, more difficulty distracting themselves from thinking about the pain, and a greater tendency to avoid doing anything that might increase their pain, such as exercise.

In 1999, Edmund Keogh and Julie Birkby in the United Kingdom investigated the relationship between AS and pain using a laboratory task that had the participant immerse a hand in ice water to induce pain. This particular task is often used in pain research because it's a safe way of inducing pain in the laboratory; obviously, people aren't required, or even permitted, to leave their hands in the ice water long enough to do any physical damage! In Keogh and Birkby's study, high-AS women reported greater sensory pain (such as more "throbbing," "stabbing," and "aching") than low-AS women in response to the ice-water immersion task. This finding was particular to women, because high-AS and low-AS men didn't show this difference in response to the task.

Subsequent research by Edmund Keogh and Louise Mansoor (2001) and Lindsay Uman and colleagues (2006) provided further evidence that anxiety sensitivity affects pain perception. In these studies, women with high AS perceived pain more negatively than those with low AS, and reported higher levels of anxiety related to the pain experience (Conrod

2006). Because high-AS people tend to be more sensitive to arousal sensations (and to misinterpret and catastrophize about these sensations), they may be predisposed to exacerbate various pain-related conditions, such as headaches, gastrointestinal pain, musculoskeletal pain, and menstrual pain (Asmundson, Vlaeyen, and Crombez 2004).

Recently, researchers have begun studying the effects of AS on women's experience of labor pain. One study conducted by Ariel Lang, John Sorrell, Carie Rodgers, and Meredith Lebeck (2006) investigated whether levels of AS taken prenatally would predict labor pains in thirty-five mothers during childbirth. Shortly after giving birth, mothers provided information about their experience of labor and delivery, including the mode of delivery (vaginal or C-section), whether anesthesia was used, duration of labor, whether labor was complicated, maximum pain during labor, duration of maximum pain, and average pain during labor. Study results indicated that AS levels, as measured by the ASI, were a significant predictor of maximum pain during labor and of sensory pain in particular.

Consider a first-time pregnant woman with a high degree of AS. She has heard "horror stories" about pain during labor, especially for first-time mothers. In fact, her own mother and friends have told her how bad the pain will be. Any information involving specific detail about childbirth reminds her about these "horror stories" and results in increased physiological responsiveness and catastrophic thoughts such as heart palpitations and thoughts that she will have unbearable pain, respectively. Together these responses lead to avoidance behavior (e.g., she does not wish to attend birthing classes because of the increase in her anxiety when talking about the birth process). When labor begins after nine months of avoidance responding, she is taken to the hospital for the delivery of her baby. Although the discomfort and pain associated with her first few contractions are not unbearable, she anticipates future contractions and begins to experience increased anxiety and fear. As her sympathetic nervous system responds, she begins to notice her heart beating faster and harder, she begins to sweat, her breathing rate changes, tightness is experienced in her throat and chest as she takes each breath, and she intermittently feels dizzy. Attentional focus towards these symptoms begins to increase as does her symptoms of anxiety. Each contraction on the way to the hospital begins to be more and more painful. She begins to think that these physiological reactions are not safe, that they could signal a problem in the delivery, that the baby is at risk, or that she won't be able to tolerate the remainder of the labor and delivery. These thoughts and beliefs increase her pain-related fear, which in turn increases her physiological reaction (e.g., heart rate, breathing, and pain), negative expectations and thoughts, and eventually lead to more avoidance behaviors. Avoidance responding at this point takes the form of a request for medication the moment she arrives at the hospital. Her request is an attempt to reduce both labor-related anxiety and pain. When the medication she receives reduces some of her pain and discomfort, her escape responding is reinforced. As her labor continues and her pain and anxiety is not entirely eliminated by the medication, she begins to fear the worst and asks that a C-section be performed.

ANXIETY SENSITIVITY AND SUBSTANCE-USE DISORDER

Emerging evidence suggests that elevated anxiety sensitivity is associated with substance-use disorders. *Substance-use disorder* refers to a maladaptive pattern of substance use, leading to clinically significant impairment or distress. Substance-use disorder is diagnosed when three (or more) of the following symptoms occur at any time in the same twelve-month period. These symptoms include tolerance (needing more and more of the substance to achieve intoxication or the desired effect) and withdrawal (needing to take the substance to relieve or avoid withdrawal symptoms).

Other symptoms include unsuccessfully trying to cut down or control substance use, plus spending a lot of time doing whatever it takes to obtain the substance (such as visiting multiple doctors or driving long distances), using the substance (for example, chain-smoking), or recovering from its effects. Important social, occupational, or recreational activities are given up or reduced because of substance use (for example, missing work or family responsibilities). And the substance use continues despite existence of a known persistent or recurrent physical or psychological problem that's probably caused or exacerbated by the substance. For example, a cocaine user might persist despite acknowledging cocaine-induced depression, or an alcoholic might continue drinking heavily despite knowing that alcohol consumption made his or her ulcer worse. The types of substances that people tend to abuse include depressants (such as alcohol and sedatives), stimulants (such as cocaine, caffeine, and nicotine), opiates (such as heroin and morphine), hallucinogens (such as marijuana and LSD), and other drugs (such as inhalants—for example, glue—and anabolic steroids).

The following sections cover what we know about anxiety sensitivity's role in abuse of commonly used drugs, namely, alcohol, benzodiazepines, nicotine, and marijuana.

Anxiety Sensitivity and Alcohol

Anxiety sensitivity is associated with reports of heavy drinking and frequent alcohol problems (Stewart, Samoluk, and MacDonald 1999). Research conducted by one of the authors of this book (Sherry Stewart) suggests that people with high levels of AS may be at risk for developing alcohol disorders. It seems that people with high AS are more responsive to alcohol's anxiety-reducing effects (MacDonald et al. 2000; Stewart and Pihl 1994). Moreover, research shows that high AS is related to people's motives for drinking. For example, people with high AS levels are more apt to report drinking alcohol for emotional relief (coping motives) and to fit in with others (conformity motives; Stewart, Zvolensky, and Eifert 2001). Both coping and conformity motives are associated with heavy drinking, drinking problems, and preoccupation with drinking (Stewart, Samoluk, and MacDonald 1999).

A recent study conducted by Florida State University researchers Norman B. Schmidt, Julia Buckner, and Meghan Keough (2007) sought to determine whether AS could actually predict the development of alcohol problems. Four hundred young, healthy adults were followed for approximately two years. Results showed that AS levels at the beginning of the study predicted later diagnoses of alcohol-use disorders. These findings support AS as a risk factor in development of alcohol-related disorders. Identifying a risk factor for alcohol abuse holds the promise of actually preventing such problems if effective prevention programs can be put in place for anxiety-sensitive people.

Anxiety Sensitivity and Benzodiazepines

Benzodiazepines are commonly prescribed for patients with anxiety disorders. Benzodiazepines (specifically Librium) were first marketed in 1957, and by the 1970s, had become one of the most prescribed medications in North America. Twenty years later, benzodiazepine dependence was identified as a major problem in patients with anxiety disorders characterized by high AS levels, such as panic disorder (Bruce et al. 1995; Otto et al. 1992). Other research (Telch, Lucas, and Nelson 1989) had found that high-AS college students report greater use of stress medications (including benzodiazepines) than low-AS college students. Ron Norton and colleagues (1997) have found that high-AS substance abusers are more likely to indicate depressant drugs (such as alcohol and benzodiazepines) as their drug of choice (52 percent) as compared with low-AS substance abusers (32 percent). Moreover, research has found that AS levels predict people's relapse to benzodiazepine use following efforts to discontinue use (Bruce et al. 1995; Stewart, Samoluk, and MacDonald 1999).

The following case study illustrates the role of AS in the treatment of a woman with comorbid anxiety disorder and benzodiazepine dependence. The client was a middle-aged, recently divorced woman with benzodiazepine dependence with comorbid panic disorder and agoraphobia. Her personality assessment indicated significantly high levels of AS. Her anxiety tended to escalate to the level of panic when she engaged in catastrophic thoughts about her anxiety symptoms and her inability to tolerate anxiety.

The client accessed her benzodiazepines through a friend, who was a physician. She showed a strong interpersonally dependent relationship with this friend, which she recognized was related to her desire to obtain access to a benzodiazepine prescription. She was quite vigilant about always having a bottle of alcohol readily available, and described how she became quite anxious if she couldn't easily get a drink. Assessment revealed that her benzodiazepine dependence was quite long-standing, with increased usage since her divorce. Her alcohol abuse had a more recent onset and appeared to be related to an attempt to further control her escalating anxiety symptoms. At the outset of treatment, she didn't recognize her benzodiazepine use pattern as a substance addiction. Rather, she saw her escalating use as an indicator that her medical treatment was failing and that she needed to find another medication to control her anxiety; this was her primary reason for referring herself to the study.

On being introduced to the idea of a personality-based model of managing her anxiety and reducing her substance misuse, she was initially quite resistant to the idea that her anxiety could be managed in ways other than through medical means (that is, drug management). But she did recognize that she had some kind of constitutional susceptibility to anxiety that was long-standing and far beyond that of others, a feature of the model that resonated for her and provided a starting point for the intervention. During the course of the brief intervention, she was guided through a cognitive exercise that required her to identify the factors (contextual, physiological, and cognitive antecedents) that preceded situations where she had experienced extreme anxiety and substance misuse. While actively engaged in this exercise, she realized that her thoughts had a catastrophic nature and were contributing to her elevated anxiety and panic attacks, and to her tendency to engage in avoidance behaviors, including benzodiazepine use and alcohol abuse. She was then taught techniques for managing her anxiety-prone thinking, such as de-catastrophizing and evaluating the probability of negative outcomes, and she practiced these techniques in other exercises with examples drawn from her own experiences. By increasing her motivation to learn to manage her anxiety and reduce her avoidance (through providing her with a reasonable model of the interplay between her two sets of symptoms), and by training her in more appropriate cognitive and behavioral skills, the intervention proved immensely beneficial for this anxiety-sensitive client. Six months after the intervention, this client showed an outcome of significant reduction in both her alcohol and benzodiazepine use.

Anxiety Sensitivity and Nicotine

Michael Zvolensky, at the University of Vermont, has conducted studies into the link between cigarette smoking and anxiety-related problems. For example, one of his studies found that cigarette smoking is more common among people with panic-related problems (panic attacks, panic disorder, and agoraphobia) than those without such problems (Zvolensky and Bernstein 2005). Other studies found that smoking increases a person's chances of having panic attacks and panic disorder in the future (Breslau and Klein 1999; Breslau, Novak, and Kessler 2004) and may simultaneously exacerbate the severity of such anxiety problems (Zvolensky et al. 2003).

AS appears to share an interesting relationship with cigarette smoking and panic-related problems (Zvolensky and Bernstein 2005). For example, recent evidence suggests that AS may influence the association between smoking and panic by fostering greater anxiety in response to smoking-related cues. In other words, high-AS smokers may respond to smoking-related cues, such as nicotine withdrawal symptoms or health impairment (for example, coughing), with greater anxiety (Zvolensky, Schmidt, and Stewart 2003). As a consequence, they may come to view these bodily cues as being personally dangerous (Zvolensky and Bernstein 2005), and this would motivate them to rid themselves of these bodily cues through any immediate means, such as by continuing smoking to relieve withdrawal symptoms.

It makes sense that an anxiety-sensitive smoker would have particular difficulties in quitting smoking since nicotine withdrawal not only involves anxiety but also a number of the bodily sensations so feared by anxiety-sensitive people. Sherry Stewart (one of the authors) and colleagues (Mullane et al. 2008) examined the relationship between AS and smoking cessation outcome in a group of smokers who took part in a structured, four-week tobacco intervention program. Results showed that AS levels were associated with higher anxiety levels during the first week of smoking cessation and poorer short-term outcome. Moreover, high-AS smokers were at greater risk of relapse by the one-month follow-up.

Anxiety Sensitivity and Marijuana

Marijuana is the most commonly used recreational drug in the world (Patton et al. 2002). Problematic use (dependence or abuse) of marijuana appears to be increasing among young adults (Compton et al. 2004). Recent studies have found that regular marijuana smokers report a withdrawal pattern when they stop using (for periods ranging from twelve hours to thirty days or longer). This pattern includes increases in anxiety, irritability, physical tension, and other related types of symptoms. The peak effects of marijuana withdrawal happen within two to four days after quitting (Budney et al. 2004).

Research has found that AS levels relate significantly to the severity of the marijuana withdrawal symptoms users report (Bonn-Miller et al. 2007). Marijuana users with high AS may fear more profoundly the unpleasant ways the withdrawal syndrome affects their thinking; for example, they fear losing control or going crazy. It's possible that these high-AS users are more apt to use marijuana to cope with distressful withdrawal symptoms (and perhaps stressors in general) than their low-AS counterparts (Bonn-Miller, Zvolensky, and Bernstein 2007). Consequently, they may worry about the negative personal consequences of withdrawal symptoms (such as losing control) because they haven't developed other ways of coping with their unpleasant moods (Zvolensky et al. 2006).

Nancy Comeau, Sherry Stewart, and Pamela Loba (2001) found that high AS levels were associated with conformity motives for alcohol and marijuana use in a large sample of adolescents. In other words, high-AS adolescents were more apt to report using alcohol or marijuana to "fit in" or avoid social disapproval. Related to this, recent studies suggest that marijuana dependence is associated with high rates of social anxiety (Buckner et al. 2007). And the National Comorbidity Study (NCS) reported that individuals with social anxiety are seven times more likely to experience marijuana-related impairment relative to the general population (Agosti, Nunes, and Levin 2002).

Case Vignette: Gavin

Gavin is a twenty-one-year-old college student with high AS and a dependence on nicotine and marijuana. Gavin started smoking cigarettes at age sixteen and, shortly thereafter, started smoking marijuana. He started smoking (both nicotine and marijuana) because it helped him relax around his peers. It allowed him to "fit in," which was important to Gavin because he found social situations difficult, to say the least. The thought of mingling with a group struck terror in Gavin. Most frightening was the prospect of appearing anxious and awkward in front of his peers and having them think he was stupid or weird. At first, marijuana seemed to relieve his anticipatory anxiety before social situations. On the other hand, it also relieved his anxiety about missing school, so his grades began to suffer. After using marijuana for a while, however, he found himself growing more anxious when under the influence. Whenever this happened, Gavin tended to avoid social situations all the more for fear of being regarded negatively for being under the influence; he might behave inappropriately while intoxicated or have to endure someone's judgment for using an illicit substance. As his use of marijuana increased over time, so did his avoidance of social situations, including school and activities with family and friends. This avoidance elevated Gavin's anxiety, which further fueled his reliance on marijuana to cope with his distress.

ANXIETY SENSITIVITY AND MENSTRUAL DISTRESS

A number of women experience menstrual distress across their reproductive lives, which is why it's somewhat surprising that relatively little research has examined the role of psychological factors that may predispose or exacerbate menstrual distress for women. Over the past ten years, Sandra Sigmon and her colleagues at the University of Maine have conducted a series of studies investigating such psychological factors, including anxiety sensitivity.

The studies by Sigmon and her colleagues suggest that AS may greatly affect women's experience and reporting of menstrual symptoms, such as cramps or headaches. These studies found that high-AS women reported more-severe menstrual symptoms than low- and moderate-AS women (Sigmon et al. 2000; Sigmon et al. 1996). To explain these findings, Sigmon and her colleagues proposed that high-AS women may be more vigilant about physical sensations, including those associated with the menstrual cycle, and consequently develop negative expectancies about them. In other words, because high-AS women are more attuned to the bodily symptoms associated with menses (such as cramps, abdominal pressure, headaches, and back pain), they're more inclined to fear the consequences of these symptoms. They may fear that the menstrual cramps will get worse and become debilitating, or that heavy blood flow will bring embarrassing spotting. This heightened fear may actually exacerbate the symptoms directly or indirectly (through increased muscle tension; Sigmon et al. 2000).

CHAPTER SUMMARY

In this chapter, we examined the role of anxiety sensitivity in a number of psychological and physical health disorders. High levels of anxiety sensitivity, particularly the psychological-concerns component of AS (such as fear of losing control when experiencing anxiety), are associated with greater levels of depression. Indeed, such psychological concerns have been described as the "depression-specific component of anxiety sensitivity" (Taylor et al. 1996, 478). There's a correlation between high AS and high health-anxiety levels. Research shows that a person can learn and reinforce hypochondriacal concerns similar to high AS in childhood. Moreover, AS appears to mediate or explain the relationship between learning history and hypochondriacal concerns. People with high AS perceive pain (including labor pain) more negatively than low-AS people. They also report higher levels of anxiety related to pain experiences and may be at higher risk for chronic pain-related conditions. Finally, research shows that AS plays a key role in development and persistence of substance-use disorders, including alcohol, benzodiazepines, nicotine, and marijuana. AS's role in substance withdrawal has implications for treatment and prevention programs. Finally, AS plays a role in how women experience menstrual symptoms.

Part III

How to Reduce
Anxiety Sensitivity

Chapter 6

Change Your Thoughts

I am an old man and have known a great many troubles,
but most of them never happened.

—Mark Twain

This chapter examines how our thoughts contribute to our anxiety experiences. In particular, we'll look at how our thoughts impact how we feel and what we do when we're anxious. The thoughts we think and the kinds of things we say to ourselves can either heighten or lessen our anxiety. As the quote from Mark Twain suggests, some of our greatest fears are imagined more than realized. Interestingly, humans are the only animals who can manage this feat (that is, scare ourselves nearly to death by thought alone). For example, we can activate our autonomic nervous system simply by imagining a disastrous outcome (for example, fainting in front of an audience or failing a test). However, if we can conjure up anxiety by thought alone, then it makes sense that we should also be able to reduce our anxiety by thought alone. In this chapter, we'll take a close look at how this is possible: how can we learn to manage our anxiety by changing the way we think? A good first step in learning to do this is to separate anxiety into its component parts—physical sensations, thoughts, feelings, and actions—and to recognize the connections among these various component parts.

RECOGNIZING CONNECTIONS AMONG PHYSICAL SENSATIONS, THOUGHTS, FEELINGS, AND ACTIONS

Anxiety specialists agree that anxiety consists of the following four major components:

1. **Physical sensations:** Muscle tension, rapid pulse, difficulty breathing, upset stomach, sweating, trembling, headaches, stomachaches, and so on

2. **Thoughts:** Thinking the worst, and being very convinced that this horrible outcome is likely to happen

3. **Feelings:** Subjective state of fear, dread, and apprehension

4. **Actions:** Actions that disrupt our performance, such as escaping from social situations, procrastinating in the face of a looming deadline, or avoiding talking to certain people because of our anxiety about how we might be evaluated

Different people experience these components of anxiety differently, depending on the situation. All four components, however, play some role in everyone's experience of anxiety. These four components are frequently closely related. For people with high anxiety sensitivity, physical sensations trigger negative thoughts, which bring about increased physical arousal, leading to feelings of apprehension and avoidance behavior.

Feedback cycles can operate as well. For example, having catastrophizing thoughts can escalate physical sensations by enhancing your subjective anxiety. And engaging in avoidance behavior can reduce your anxiety in the short term (which is reinforcing) but maintain it or even increase it in the longer term, because you aren't sticking around to learn that your catastrophic thoughts were unwarranted. It's the interaction of these four components that results in the spiral into extreme anxiety, fear, or panic.

PHYSICAL SENSATIONS

I feel dizzy!
My heart's racing!
I can't breathe!
My face is red!

THOUGHTS

I'm going to die!
This is terrible!
I can't handle this!
They're laughing at me!

FEELINGS

Fear
Dread
Panic
Anxiety
Apprehension

ACTIONS

Escape/Avoidance   Positive Self-talk
Distraction   Relaxation
Drugs/Alcohol   Breathing
Physical Exercise

To better understand the relationship among these four components, consider the following questions:

1. **What if you walked into a room and everyone stopped talking? What would you think? How would you feel? What would you do?** When asked this question, anxiety-sensitive people often respond that they would think that the others had been talking negatively about them. As a result, they say they would feel bad and perhaps blush, grow silent, withdraw, or even leave. However, what if the people in the room had been speaking positively about you? What if it was merely coincidence that they stopped speaking when you entered the room, and they hadn't talked about you at all? Consider another scenario: what if it was your birthday and you suspected that the people in the room were planning to surprise you in some way? How would you feel then? In this case, you might feel happy, excited, or flattered and would likely have no trouble approaching the group. These are examples of how what we think can influence how we feel and what we do.

2. **Can you think of examples of when your actions affected your thoughts or feelings?** For example, perhaps you've noticed that when you engage in physical activity (such as a brisk walk, run, working out at the gym, or playing a sport), you think differently and feel better. Recently, a group of German researchers demonstrated why we might feel better after sustained exercise. By using brain-imaging techniques, Henning Boecker and his colleagues (2008) investigated the source of the "runner's high," a positive mood state (even euphoria) induced by running and other high-intensity physical activities. Boecker's group performed positron emission tomography (PET scans) on ten athletes while they were at rest and after two hours of running. They found a direct relationship between the level of euphoria after running and the release of endogenous opioids. *Endogenous opioids* are substances that are naturally produced by our bodies ("endogenous" means "produced within the body"). Drugs such as heroin and morphine are referred to as *exogenous opioids*. The reason these drugs affect us so powerfully is that they bind to the same receptor sites in the brain as our endogenous opioids. Endogenous opioids impact our reactions to pain, regulate vital functions such as hunger and thirst, and are involved in mood control and immune response. Endogenous opioids also impact the functioning of the hypothalamic-pituitary-adrenal (HPA) axis, which regulates our

response to stress (Olson, Olson, and Kastin 1996). The 2008 study by Boecker and colleagues demonstrates a clear link between actions (in this case, physical exercise) and feelings or mood (in this case, euphoria), and makes clear the underlying events in the brain that explain this link (in this case, endogenous opiate release).

3. **Can you think of examples of when your actions affected your physical sensations?** Consider times when you experienced symptoms of anxiety, or perhaps pain, and were able to reduce these symptoms, at least in the short term, by resting, relaxing, or doing some diaphragmatic breathing.

4. **Can you think of examples of when your thoughts affected your physical sensations?** An abundance of evidence points to the role of thoughts in modulating our response to pain. For example, Michael Sullivan performed extensive research into the role of catastrophizing about pain. *Catastrophizing* is thinking that the worst will happen, dwelling on the prospect that it will happen, and feeling helpless to do anything about it. High levels of pain catastrophizing are associated with a more-intense pain experience, more pronounced displays of pain behavior, heightened emotional distress, and greater disability (Sullivan et al. 2001, Keefe et al. 2004, and Thorn et al. 2004). The relation between catastrophizing and pain has been observed in patients with low back pain, rheumatoid arthritis, dental procedures, and whiplash injuries, as well as in samples of varsity athletes and people without pain conditions who participated in experimental pain procedures (Sullivan et al. 2001). Moreover, there's growing evidence that pain-related fear, including fear of pain, physical activity, and reinjury, may be more disabling for back-pain patients than the pain itself (Crombez et al. 1999).

5. **Can you think of examples of when your physical sensations affected your actions?** This is particularly relevant for people with high AS. It's the physical sensations associated with anxiety that trigger their catastrophic thinking. The catastrophic thinking increases their anxiety, prompting them to escape or avoid as a means to reduce the anxiety. But can changing our thoughts alter how we feel or what course of action we take in a stressful situation? Psychologist and philosopher William James (1842–1910) thought so. According to James, "As you think, so shall you be." James's significant interest in the impact of thinking on emotional states was very likely driven by his personal experience with panic attacks and related somatoform complaints (review chapter 5; Stossel 1998).

PRINCIPLES AND STRATEGIES FOR OVERCOMING ANXIETY SENSITIVITY

Consider the following scenario: *You're all alone in a strange house and hear an unusual sound. What do you think? What do you do?*

Some people would start to concentrate on the sound and grow more frightened by the minute as they imagined the many frightening possibilities that it could represent. This is similar to having high AS and turning up the volume on the physiological sensations associated with anxiety. Other people, perhaps less sensitive to strange sounds in the night, might remind themselves that old houses make lots of sounds. They might tell themselves that they wouldn't have even heard the sound had they been engrossed in conversation or watching their favorite television shows, and would dismiss the sound and avoid focusing on it any further. This is similar to turning down the volume on the physiological sensations associated with anxiety.

The point is that we augment (turn up) or reduce (turn down) our attention to such physiological sensations depending on what kinds of things we say to ourselves when we experience these sensations. There are techniques, however, that can help us challenge the kinds of thoughts or statements that we tend to say to ourselves, especially those that occur when we feel the emotions of fear and anxiety. This is what we'll learn in this chapter. The techniques described in this chapter are derived from the work of Patricia Conrod (2000) and colleagues (Conrod et al. 2000) and are reproduced here with permission of the author.

1. To identify our thoughts when we feel fearful and anxious. What kinds of thoughts lead us to feel fear and anxiety?

2. To recognize the connections among physical sensations, feelings, thoughts, and actions.

3. To challenge our own thinking. By challenging our own self-statements—the ways we tend to talk to ourselves when we experience anxiety—we can interrupt the cycle of anxiety and panic, and thereby reduce our risk for panic attacks and other forms of distress.

Identify Dysfunctional Automatic Thoughts

Dysfunctional automatic thoughts are specific self-statements that occur so automatically that you're probably not even aware of them. The first thing we need to learn is how to identify and monitor the dysfunctional thoughts that lead to anxiety and panic. We might say to ourselves, "I don't tell myself anything when I panic; it just comes out of the blue." It's important to realize that we have different levels of awareness of our own thoughts. Sometimes we're well aware that we're thinking very frightening things, and other times the information we give ourselves can be very automatic. The focus of our automatic thoughts may differ from one situation to another. For example, we may be mostly afraid of embarrassment in one situation and mostly afraid of being alone or in danger in another situation. Sometimes we have to search very hard for the particular thoughts that are present in a given situation. For example, identifying the thought as "I felt terrible" may not be particularly helpful in learning to better manage our anxiety, because it's too broad and doesn't tell us anything useful about what we really fear will happen in a given situation. We must try to analyze our thinking even more to get at the predictions we're making about what we believe will happen.

What do we picture happening? What do we think could happen as a result of feeling anxious? Once we can identify specific dysfunctional thoughts, we're in a position to directly challenge the thoughts. Stopping at the point of "I'm afraid" doesn't allow us to use specific techniques to change the way we think. Therefore, it's very important to pursue the thought by continuing to question it until we've identified what we're saying to ourselves about what might happen to us.

EXPLORE YOUR AUTOMATIC THOUGHTS

Go back to a specific episode of anxiety that you experienced within the past couple of weeks. Visualize the experience exactly, as if it were happening right now: Where are you? Who is present? What's happening? What are you doing? How do you feel? What are you thinking? What exactly are you saying to yourself in this situation?

Zoom in on your thoughts in that situation. What were the major kinds of thoughts going through your mind just *before*, *during*, and *after* the episodes of anxiety or panic? Are your descriptions very general, such as "I felt terrible" or "I felt anxious"? If so, try to remember the event exactly as it occurred and try to think of the exact words you said to yourself at that time. What was going through your head? What were the images crossing your mind? Why was the situation so terrible? What did you think could happen? What would it have meant if the consequence you imagined had actually happened?

Following is a guide for exploring your thoughts so you can identify them in more specific ways. Let's try an example.

1. **Recall a specific incident in which you became anxious. Write a brief description of it:** *I had finally secured a job interview. The job sounded perfect for me: more money and better hours than my last job. I was really excited about being called for the interview—at first. As the time approached, however, I grew increasingly anxious about the interview. I began to question my credentials for the job and anticipated the interview going badly. I thought that they might ask why I thought I was a suitable candidate for the job and I wouldn't have an answer. I anticipated turning red and shaking in the interview and that the interviewers would wonder what was wrong with me. Certainly, they wouldn't give me the job. The night before the interview, I couldn't sleep. The morning of the interview, I felt sick to my stomach and had a strong desire to call in sick or even cancel the interview altogether.*

2. **Specify at least two thoughts you had in association with the event.**

   Thought #1: *I can't do this.*

   Thought #2: *I feel terrible.*

Thought #3: *I don't need this job.*

3. **In your own words, define the terms you used previously to describe your thoughts. First write the terms and then their definitions.**

   Term: *I can't do this.*

   Definition: *It's too hard for me to do this. I'll blow the interview.*

   Term: *I feel terrible.*

   Definition: *Panicky, sick to my stomach, heart skipping beats, a bit disoriented*

   Term: *I don't need this job.*

   Definition: *If I feel so bad about going to the interview, this job can't be good for me.*

4. **Using more specific terms, write what your thoughts were in association with the event.**

   Thought #1: *I find it hard to meet new people at the best of times but especially if they're interviewing me for a job. I don't do well in interview situations. I never know how to prepare for the interview, what to wear, or how to respond to the questions. I hate people asking me questions and scrutinizing my behavior, which is what they'll be doing. I always feel so stupid.*

   Thought #2: *Just thinking about going through the interview makes me feel sick to my stomach. I can feel my face getting red thinking about the humiliation of looking stupid when I can't answer the questions. I'm apt to get sick or pass out in the room. The interviewers are sure to notice my face getting red, and they'll think I'm very strange.*

   Thought #3: *If going for the interview is this stressful, then the job probably isn't right for me. I'll wait until another job comes along, because I won't get this one anyway. I don't have enough experience for this particular job. In any case, my anxiety will get the best of me and I'll blow the interview.*

Now, think of an example from your own personal experience and proceed through the steps.

1. **Recall a specific incident in which you became anxious. Write a brief description of it:**

   _____

   _____

2. **Specify at least two thoughts you had in association with the event.**

   Thought #1: _____

   Thought #2: _____

3. **In your own words, define the terms you used previously to describe your thoughts. First write the terms and then their definitions.**

   Term: _____

   Definition: _____

4. **Using more specific terms, write what your thoughts were in association with the event.**

   Thought #1: _____

   Thought #2: _____

Common Misinterpretations Leading to Anxiety

Generally, there are two types of errors in processing information that influence the anxiety cycle in stressful situations such as going to a job interview. These errors in thinking can be conceptualized as types of *automatic thoughts*. Automatic thoughts tend to inflate the significance of the information being processed. The first error we tend to make is to catastrophize; in other words, we focus in on the worst-case scenario as a potential outcome of the situation. The second type of error we're inclined to make is to overestimate the probability that something catastrophic (worst-case scenario) will occur.

Learning to address these thinking errors requires that we go through four steps. At each step, we have to ask ourselves the following specific questions:

✦ What do you think will happen? What's the worst-case scenario?

✦ What's the probability? How likely is it to happen?

✦ What if it does happen? So what?

✦ What else could you think?

What Do You Think Will Happen? What's the Worst-Case Scenario?

The first type of thinking error that people make when feeling anxious or frightened is called *catastrophic thinking*. For example, let's return to the scenario we discussed earlier: you're alone in a strange house and hear an odd sound. You might begin to think that the house is haunted or perhaps the chainsaw-wielding "Leatherface" character from the popular 1974 horror film *The Texas Chainsaw Massacre* has come to visit. Even if you don't think of ghosts or scary-movie characters, you might begin to think that it's someone intent on doing you harm. Now, unnecessary anxiety and fear develop by viewing the event as dangerous, insufferable, or catastrophic when, in all probability, it's not. Following are some typical kinds of catastrophic thoughts related to anxiety-provoking situations:

✦ "If my heart keeps racing like this, it could wear out."

✦ "I feel like I'm losing control over my mental faculties."

✦ "If other people noticed my anxiety and panicky feelings, it would be terrible and I could never face them again."

The problem with this type of thinking is that people respond with even more anxiety and fear, without ever stopping to examine the truth of these kinds of statements. If you stop to realistically examine the actual event, it's usually not as catastrophic as you first thought. For example, if you fainted from hyperventilation, it wouldn't be such a terrible event, because fainting is actually an adaptive mechanism designed to reestablish balance in the body. The worst that can happen from fainting (providing you don't fall on a hard surface) is a brief feeling of disorientation after regaining consciousness. Ask yourself, *what if* you did faint in front of the class? What would happen? What would you think of someone else if they fainted in front of the class?

What's the Probability? How Likely Is It to Happen?

The second type of thinking error is called *probability overestimation*. This type of thinking can result in an incorrect prediction of "how likely" it is that a certain outcome will occur. This thinking error can cause a person to jump to a negative conclusion that causes much anxiety. Instead, a person should ask herself or himself, "What are the chances? What are the chances that the worst-case scenario will happen?" Think back to situations when you were anxious or panicked and thought something terrible would happen. Now ask yourself whether any of the feared catastrophic events actually occurred. What does the evidence from your own experience tell you?

Consider this scenario: You're a healthy eighteen-year-old woman with no history of heart problems. As you prepare to write an exam, your heart starts racing. Your heart beats so fast it seems to skip beats. Your chest begins to feel tight; you start to feel as if you can't breathe; you grow convinced that you'll have a heart attack. How likely is it that a young woman with no history of heart problems will have a heart attack? How often have you heard of eighteen-year-old women having heart attacks? How likely is it? What are the chances?

You might say, "Yes, I know. But the possibility of something catastrophic happening is still frightening." It's common for people to find ways of thinking that allow them to continue overestimating the probability of a catastrophic event rather than realize the inaccuracy of the original prediction. Indeed, as humans, we're predisposed to seek reasons or evidence that confirms our thinking and beliefs, so we tend to disregard or place less weight on disconfirming reasons or evidence against these thoughts and beliefs. This is known as the *confirmation bias*. For example, someone might say, "If I hadn't gone to the emergency room, I don't know what would've happened." In other words, real evidence (for example, "I had predicted that I'd have a heart attack, but in fact, my prediction didn't come true; I didn't have a heart attack") is ignored or distorted to fit the belief that there was, in fact, danger present. Because medical practitioners are bound by law and ethics to conduct an assessment when someone presents at an emergency room, this too is used as confirmatory evidence (for example, "The doctor thought my symptoms were serious enough to do an EKG"). The truth is that, in this example, the person survived the panic or anxiety episode because there was no real danger.

Next, we'll look at how to challenge our automatic thoughts to keep our anxiety at bay.

Challenge Your Thinking

As psychologist William James said, "The greatest weapon against stress is our ability to choose one thought over another." To gain mastery over your anxiety, it's very important that you learn how to challenge automatic thinking, such as catstrophizing and overestimating the probability. To do this effectively, we need to collect evidence. We must resist the confirmation bias and look for information that disconfirms our fears rather than confirms them. We must closely examine our thoughts to evaluate their accuracy and logic. We must learn to choose the rational thought over the fear-inducing thought. The most helpful technique for evaluating a thought is to examine the evidence that supports it.

In a sense, you need to consider yourself a scientist who runs "mini-experiments" designed to gather data to test out whether your thoughts are correct. It's important to conduct a logical analysis of your thoughts when they first enter your mind. To do so, first remind yourself that just because you're thinking about losing control, dying, and so on doesn't mean you will. Instead of treating those thoughts as reasons to become more frightened, evaluate them objectively. Let's go back to the two common thinking errors that lead to anxiety so we can learn some techniques to challenge these thinking errors.

Examining the Evidence

The way to challenge overestimations is to *examine the evidence* for your probability judgments.

Remember to treat your thoughts as guesses rather than facts. Before you make a judgment, examine the evidence for your prediction. Your interpretation of any given situation represents one of many possible interpretations. It is important to explore alternative interpretations, especially given the knowledge that when we're anxious, we tend to be biased in our interpretations. The goal is not to remove anxiety concerning real threats but to minimize your thinking errors in situations where there's no real threat.

To evaluate the evidence for a prediction, ask yourself:

✦ What are the true odds of this happening?

✦ Has this ever happened before?

✦ What's the evidence that it won't happen?

Asking yourself these questions requires that you consider all the facts and all the evidence before predicting the likelihood of something's happening. For example, a friend may act in a hostile or cold manner. You assume that he's displeased with you, yet you've overlooked the possibility that he may feel angry with someone else or has merely had a bad day. In terms of anxiety sensations, you may assume that a tingling in your left arm is a sign of a heart attack, overlooking the fact that you're in good health and have experienced the tingling many times before without suffering a heart attack. It's also possible that you're making negative predictions on the basis of a very limited set of past examples. For instance, you may predict that you'll become anxious because you've become anxious in similar situations before. However, you may overlook many instances in which you weren't anxious in those situations. You may, in fact, confuse low probabilities with high probabilities or think that negative outcomes are certain rather than just possible. The base rate for events that result in disastrous consequences is very low; that is, they occur quite infrequently—fortunately! But, because these events are highly memorable, we tend to misjudge how often they occur.

De-catastrophizing

De-catastrophizing means imagining the consequences of the worst-case scenario and then gathering information about the threat to critically evaluate the true danger. You can conduct this kind of analysis with events that are both likely to happen (such as shaking when you feel anxious in a public situation) and unlikely to happen (such as fainting when panicked). If the worst that's considered likely to happen is death or loss of a significant other, then de-catastrophizing may not be effective, because for most people, it's not always appropriate to say that it's not so bad to die or lose someone very close to you. Fears of death or loss are generally more appropriate to the analysis of overestimation; that is, how likely is it that you'll die the next time you panic and how likely is it that you'll lose someone close to you? It's worth noting, however, that in some cases it could be very helpful to more closely examine what would be so awful about the possibility of dying. An example is the case of a woman with hypochondriasis who believed that leaving her children motherless would be horrible because nobody would care for them as she did. In this case, examining the underlying meaning of her fear of death helped her identify and know how to address the specific concern. In most cases of predictions of death or loss of a loved one, however, challenging the probability overestimation is the best first step.

The next time you panic or consider an upcoming situation about which you're worried, ask yourself: what's the worst possible thing that could happen? What if you did faint when you panicked? What if you did look very shaky when speaking to others? Your first reaction to these questions might be something like "That would be awful" or "I couldn't stand it." However, when you think carefully and critically about these assumptions, you'll find that you have prematurely assumed them to be catastrophic. If you analyze your thinking, you'll probably find that, in actuality, you could tolerate any misfortune that happened. It's only the statement "I couldn't stand it" that creates the anxiety, that makes us think we couldn't manage.

De-catastrophizing can be summed up in one phrase: so what? What if the worst-case scenario did happen? What would you do? Could you survive? What would you do if you saw others faint, shake, or turn red? What would you say to others if they expressed similar fears?

Substituting with Reasonable Thoughts: What Else Could You Think?

It's important to learn how to replace your negative thoughts with more reasonable, helpful thoughts, because without a set of alternatives, it's difficult to resist falling back on your previously established thinking errors. To start off, it can help to simply write down the alternatives (even if you don't yet completely believe them) or repeat them in your head a couple of times. If you practice these alternative thoughts, eventually they'll become more automatic and will come to you almost as easily as your previously established negative thoughts. Throughout this process, you'll also need to explore the alternatives and reshape them so that they become thoughts that you believe and so that they can be integrated into your system of thinking about yourself and the world around you.

Let's try to challenge some thoughts commonly associated with anxiety and panic. Then we'll try to challenge some of the thoughts you have when you feel anxious or when you anticipate a panic attack. Remember, after you've challenged a thought, provide yourself with an alternative so you can replace the automatic thought with a more reasonable and helpful way of thinking. The following exercises have been adapted with permission from the author, Patricia Conrod (2000; Conrod et al. 2000)).

MODIFY YOUR SELF-STATEMENTS: WHAT ARE THE CHANCES?

Thoughts	Examine the Evidence
I could faint the next time I panic.	What are the chances of fainting? What is the probability on a 0- to 100-point scale? How many times have I actually fainted in the past?
I could have a car accident when I feel dizzy.	How many times have I felt dizzy when driving? How many times have I had a car accident when feeling dizzy?
If I'm left alone, I'll really lose it and go crazy.	What has happened to me in the past when I've been left alone? Have I ever tested out my prediction to see what would happen if I were alone? I might feel anxious, but what evidence do I have that I would go crazy?

The pains in my chest must mean that I'm having a heart attack.	What's the evidence against this possibility? What were the results from my last medical checkup? How many times have I felt pain in my chest? Have I ever had a heart attack? How likely is it for a person of my age and sex to have a heart attack? (Conrod 2000; Conrod et al. 2000)

Now you try challenging your own overestimation errors:

Thoughts	Examine the Evidence

MODIFY YOUR SELF-STATEMENTS: WHAT IF? SO WHAT?

CATASTROPHIZING ERRORS What If?	DE-CATASTROPHIZING So What?
What if I did faint in front of a lot of people? That would be terrible!	If I fainted, there would be a reason and my body would use fainting to reestablish balance. The people around me wouldn't know what was going on. They'd try to help. What if they did think I fainted because I was nervous? So what? I'd still survive.
What if I shook terribly when talking to other people? What if they thought I was crazy?	Do I know these people? If they were strangers, would it matter what they thought? If they were friends, no matter what they thought at that time, we would still be friends. In any case, embarrassment isn't fatal.
What if I were trapped in the elevator for an hour and panicked the whole time? I couldn't cope!	Yes, I might feel anxious for the whole time, but what else could happen? So what if I were anxious? It wouldn't last forever.
My whole life is terrible. I can't go on. One day I'll just collapse and that will be the end.	Let's say I did reach a point of physical and mental exhaustion, and collapsed, meaning that I'd become withdrawn and immobile. After a period of recovery, I'd be back up again. I'd survive. (Conrod 2000; Conrod et al. 2000)

Now you try challenging your own catastrophizing errors:

CATASTROPHIZING ERRORS What If?	DE-CATASTROPHIZING So What?

WHAT ELSE CAN I THINK?

Now, let's try putting it all together. What if your heart starts racing and you begin to think you are having a heart attack? As you've learned, if you continue to think that way, your anxiety will increase and could lead to a panic attack. What are the chances that you are having a panic attack versus a heart attack? What could you say to yourself to reduce your anxiety? What if you said to yourself, "It's unlikely that I'm having a heart attack. This is probably anxiety, and the best thing I can do for myself right now is to breathe and try to relax. I shouldn't fight my body but should work with it. I can just ride it through."

What if you thought you were going to faint in front of the whole class? What are the chances that you would faint? What could you say to yourself instead of thinking the worst? What if you said to yourself, "This is just part of being anxious. This feeling will pass; it can't last forever. Fainting is actually rare in panic attacks. The best thing I can do is just relax, breathe, and go with the feeling (ride the wave) rather than fight it. If I don't fight to control the sensations, they won't get worse?" It might be helpful to know that a relaxed body is less apt to faint. Fainting is caused by a sudden and significant drop in blood pressure. During a panic attack, blood pressure actually rises; in other words, it does the opposite of what leads to fainting. It's extremely difficult to faint during a panic attack. The fear of fainting is more prevalent and is related to the symptoms of dizziness and light-headedness during a panic attack. These symptoms are very uncomfortable but not dangerous, and don't lead to fainting. Diaphragmatic breathing can restore a sense of calmness and clarity. We'll learn all about diaphragmatic breathing in the next chapter.

CHAPTER SUMMARY

According to a Japanese proverb, "Fear is only as deep as the mind allows." In this chapter, we looked at how we can limit how much fear our mind allows. We've learned how to identify those kinds of thoughts that increase our anxiety: catastrophizing and overestimating the probability. We also learned how to challenge these thoughts by examining the evidence and modifying our self-statements. You now have a method for challenging your anxious thinking. The next time you start to experience those telltale sensations of mounting anxiety, ask yourself the following questions:

1. What do I think will happen? What's the worst-case scenario?

2. What are the chances it will happen? How likely is it?

3. What if it does happen? So what?

4. What else could I think?

Chapter 7

Change Your Behavior

Nothing diminishes anxiety faster than action.

—Walter Anderson

In chapter 6 we looked at the role of our thoughts in our anxiety experiences and how changing our thoughts can change the way we feel and behave. We learned that anxiety sensitivity has physical, cognitive, emotional, and behavioral components. We may fear the physical sensations of anxiety; exacerbate the fear by thinking in certain ways; feel the mounting fear and apprehension; and then respond by avoiding, distracting, or escaping. One form of escape that some people use is drinking alcohol or using drugs, but this form of escape can be very dangerous. Of course, as we learned in chapter 6, there are better things we can do to manage our anxiety than engage in avoidance or escapist behaviors; one is to change our thinking. This chapter more closely examines our behavior and how changing our behavior can bring important benefits. For example, changing our behavior can positively affect physical sensations, moods, and even thoughts.

USING AVOIDANCE AS A
COPING MECHANISM

*We must face what we fear; that is the case of the core
of the restoration of health.*

—Max Lerner

Anxiety tends to assume a self-perpetuating cycle, fueled largely by distorted ways of thinking and escape or avoidance behavior. Consider the following example: Gail has severe anxiety, particularly when it comes to speaking in public. Throughout her university career, she managed to choose her courses so that she wasn't required to do any oral presentations. At times, this meant that she couldn't take courses of interest to her; however, in her mind, that disadvantage paled in comparison to the benefit of not having to stand in front of her classmates. Recently, however, one of her professors introduced the requirement of a class presentation. As the time for her presentation approaches, she grows increasingly anxious. The night before, she imagines all sorts of terrible possibilities that could befall her when she stands in front of the class. The more anxious she gets, the more catastrophic her thoughts become; and the more catastrophic her thoughts, the more anxious she gets. Then, as if to make matters worse, she starts to feel sick. She convinces herself that she can't do the presentation if she's sick. The next morning, she sends an e-mail to her professor citing ill health. Sending the e-mail and avoiding having to give the presentation relieves Gail's anxiety and therefore reinforces her avoidance behavior. This means that the odds that she'll avoid presentations in the future have increased, because she feels so relieved from avoiding this time around. After several such scenarios, Gail could get stuck in an anxiety-avoidance cycle that will be very difficult to break.

✦ Has something like this happened to you? _____

✦ Can you think of events or situations that you avoided?_____

✦ In retrospect, did your avoidance behavior actually increase your fear of the activity in the long run? _____

Some people cope with severe anxiety or panic attacks by avoiding situations in which they might occur. Typically, the avoided places or situations are those where escape might be difficult or where help might be unavailable in the event of extreme anxiety or a panic attack (such as at a grocery store or a church). There are other, milder types of avoidance as well, such as avoiding coffee, exercise, anger, or sex. These are all methods that people, especially those with high AS, use to avoid experiencing the physical sensations that they often misinterpret as being dangerous. Many of these methods help people get through a panic attack but do nothing to prevent future attacks (Conrod 2000; Conrod et al. 2000).

Case Vignette from Clinical Case Studies

In a recent issue of the journal Clinical Case Studies, *British clinician Karen Addy (2007) describes the case of a seventy-five-year-old woman whose anxiety-related avoidance behavior posed a significant risk to her health. The woman suffered from chronic obstructive pulmonary disease (COPD), which is a condition characterized by airflow obstruction. COPD is progressive and usually irreversible. It produces symptoms of fatigue and breathlessness from reduced lung capacity and associated lack of oxygen in the blood. Respiratory infections are common. According to Addy, people with COPD often avoid physical exercise, because they fear it will worsen their condition. Inactivity, however, can expedite the disease process, reducing the patient's quality of life and life expectancy. A psychological assessment revealed that the woman met the diagnostic criteria for both depression and an anxiety disorder with panic attacks. She was reluctant to take any further medications but agreed to twelve sessions of psychotherapy of an adapted cognitive behavioral treatment designed to increase her tolerance to her physical symptoms and reduce her avoidance of physical activities. Treatment included education about anxiety and avoidance, scheduling of behavioral activities (such as alternating intervals of walking with rest and light housework) and mindfulness-based relaxation combined with thought-acceptance techniques (Segal, Williams, and Teasdale 2002). This woman's program was deemed to have been successful based on her reduced avoidance behavior, enhanced quality of life, and increased self-esteem.*

USING DISTRACTION AS A COPING MECHANISM

Distraction refers to deliberately focusing on neutral or pleasant thoughts, or engaging in activities that divert attention away from intrusive worries and toward more positive directions (Broderick 2005). Distraction is not the same as avoidance because it's intended to help you stay in the stressful situation, not to opt out of it. Distraction has been found to effectively reduce distress across a range of conditions (Harvey and Payne 2002; Fauerbach et al. 2002). Indeed, many people employ distraction to cope with fear-inducing situations. For example, when we feel ourselves becoming anxious, we might play loud music; play counting games (such as counting ceiling tiles); try to imagine ourselves somewhere else; ask a companion to talk about something else; place cold, wet towels on our faces; or breathe into a paper bag (Conrod 2000). In some specific situations, distraction can be a very effective technique. For someone who's afraid of flying, distraction (such as reading a book) can be a very effective technique for disregarding the anxiety-provoking thoughts, sights, and sounds associated with flying.

But like avoidance, distraction techniques are not helpful in the long run, because they don't change the fear of having future panic attacks. Indeed, whereas these techniques might've allowed us to escape from feeling anxiety or having a panic attack in the past, the problem is that we can come to depend on them, actually becoming more anxious without them.

USING DRUGS AND ALCOHOL AS A COPING MECHANISM

Whereas some forms of distraction are harmless, others—such as using alcohol, nicotine, and anti-anxiety medications to cope with anxiety—can be extremely dangerous. Researchers estimate that one-third to one-half of people with drug and alcohol problems began the cycle of abuse and dependence by "self-medicating" their anxiety or panic (Bolton et al. 2006; Conrod 2000). Using these drugs is so dangerous because, although they work well in the short term, tolerance and dependence can develop quickly. Tolerance means that the person requires more of the drug to experience the desired anxiety-reducing effects. As the person increases his or her consumption, the anxiety-reducing properties of the alcohol or drugs diminish. When this occurs, anxiety increases as does the person's risk for addiction. The person can become so reliant on the drug that he or she cannot cope with anxiety without the drug.

Studies show that anxiety disorders often co-occur with substance-use disorders (Watt et al. 2008). About 15 to 30 percent of people with anxiety disorders also suffer from alcohol dependence (Barlow 1997), and 25 to 45 percent of those with alcohol dependence also suffer from anxiety disorders (Kushner et al. 2005). These rates are considerably higher than those of the general population. One study, which included more than twenty thousand respondents from five communities in the United States, found that alcoholics were significantly more apt to have an anxiety disorder than nonalcoholics (19.4 percent versus 13.1 percent) and that individuals with an anxiety disorder had a 50 percent increased risk of being diagnosed with an alcohol-use disorder at some point in their lifetimes (Regier, Narrow, and Rae 1990). Interestingly, women with either an anxiety disorder or a substance-use disorder are approximately 30 percent more likely than men to have the coexisting disorder (Kushner et al. 2008).

A number of proposals have been suggested to explain the relationship between anxiety and substance-use disorders (for example, Watt et al. 2008). One explanation is that substance abuse precedes and contributes to development of anxiety disorders (Conrod and Stewart 2005; Stewart and Conrod 2003, 2008). For example, chronic use of alcohol and other drugs may promote anxiety disorders due to damage to the stress-response system (McNaughton 2008). Another explanation is that anxiety problems precede and contribute to substance abuse. In this case, anxiety disorders may promote use of drugs and alcohol as the anxious person attempts to self-medicate the anxiety symptoms. Self-medication could operate in two ways: (1) reduction of anxiety symptoms by depressants such as alcohol or (2) enhancement of psychological well-being by stimulants (for example, cocaine) or hallucinogens (for example, ecstasy) (Kushner et al. 2008). As a personality style, anxiety sensitivity is associated with sensitivity to anxiety-reducing effects of alcohol (MacDonald et al. 2000; Stewart and Pihl 1994) and to higher levels of coping and conformity motives for drinking (Stewart, Zvolensky, and Eifert 2001).

Researchers generally agree that the coexistence of anxiety and substance-use disorders can develop in a number of ways. Anxiety can lead to substance-use disorder through self-medication; on the other hand, using anxiety-reducing drugs (such as alcohol) can result in dependence and withdrawal that generates significant anxiety (McNaughton 2008). Whatever the mechanism, the results can be devastating. And for most people with both problems, a vicious cycle develops wherein one problem sustains and even worsens the other in the long term.

If you drink or take drugs to control your anxiety, you should make every effort to stop or cut back as soon as possible. Ask your family physician or mental health professional for help if you'd like to stop. If you're physically dependent on the drug, withdrawal should be monitored medically. Your family physician or mental health professional can help you devise a plan for coming off the drugs slowly to lessen withdrawal symptoms. In addition, working on managing your anxiety through the program in this book may actually help you better manage your withdrawal symptoms in coming off the drugs (see Stewart and Conrod 2008).

How do you know if you're drinking too much or relying too heavily on other drugs for relief of anxiety? Some of the warning signs of potential addiction are as follows. Circle Y for yes or N for no:

Y N   When you're worried about something or feeling stressed, the first thing you think about is using your drug of choice (for example, having a drink).

Y N   You find it increasingly difficult to cope with anxiety without the use of the drug.

Y N   You find that you need more of the drug than previously to experience relief from anxiety.

Y N   You feel guilty about your drug use.

Y N   You have made efforts to cut back on your drug use and have not been successful.

Y N   Your drug use is interfering with your functioning at work, at school, in relationships, and so forth.

Y   N   People who care for you have expressed concern or complained about your drug use.

If you responded yes to any of these questions, consider talking to a professional (such as a family physician or addictions counselor) about your drug use.

What can we do instead of escape, avoid, distract, and drink? We can modify our response to anxiety by modifying our behavior and learning "to be in anxiety." Recall Kierkegaard's quote from chapter 1: "He … who has learned rightly *to be in anxiety* has learned the most important thing." Kierkegaard was a philosopher, not a mental health professional, and his concept of anxiety referred more to feelings of guilt and sin than our current understanding of the term. Nonetheless, his assertion that we must learn "to be in anxiety" is both relevant and appropriate to anxiety management, perhaps especially to high-AS management.

MODIFYING BEHAVIOR TO EFFECTIVELY COPE WITH ANXIETY

One of the ways we can learn "to be in anxiety" (that is, reduce our fears of the sensations associated with anxiety) is to expose ourselves to the feared sensations. *Interoceptive exposure* refers to repeated exposure to feared physical sensations (such as increased respiration and heart rate) as a means of reducing the fear of those sensations. Interoceptive exposure exercises include hyperventilation (overbreathing), spinning around while standing or while sitting in a swivel chair, and breathing through a narrow straw. Such exercises have been demonstrated effective in treating panic attacks and panic disorder, both as part of a broader cognitive behavioral program (for example, Barlow et al. 2000) and as a useful intervention in their own right (for example, Craske et al. 1997). Interoceptive exposure exercises are intended to direct anxiety-sensitive people to attend to their feared sensations, challenge their catastrophic thoughts about the sensations, and accept their anxiety experiences so that the sensations of physiological arousal no longer provoke panic or avoidance behaviors (see Otto, Powers, and Fischmann 2005).

The goal of interoceptive exposure is habituation. *Habituation* refers to decreased response to a stimulus after repeated presentations. For example, we often find it hard to sleep in a novel environment because we're sensitive to the new sounds. After a time, however, we become accustomed to the sounds and pay less attention to the noise, and our response diminishes so that we sleep better. This diminished response is an example of habituation.

There are a number of interoceptive exposure techniques that mental health professionals use to help clients habituate to their feared physical sensations. Some examples of these techniques include hyperventilating or overbreathing for 1 minute, shaking your head from side to side for 30 seconds, spinning around (while standing) for 1 minute, holding your breath for 30 seconds, breathing through a drinking straw for 2 minutes, and placing your head between your knees for 30 seconds and then lifting it quickly to the normal position (see the following table). Each of these techniques is intended to have the anxious person face the physical sensations that make him or her anxious (thereby reducing avoidance behavior) and replace mistaken beliefs about the consequences of these sensations.

Martin Antony and colleagues (2006) examined the relationship between fear of particular physical sensations (physical-concerns items on the Anxiety Sensitivity Index) and reported levels of fear and panic following specific exercises that triggered the most intense physical reactions. Participants included people with panic disorder and nonclinical controls. As expected, results showed that people with panic disorder responded more strongly than controls to symptom-induction exercises. The exercises that produced the most fear included spinning, hyperventilation, breathing through a straw, and using a tongue depressor. Closer examination revealed that the ASI items most strongly associated with a fear response while breathing through a straw were "Unusual body sensations scare me" and "It scares me when I feel shaky." The ASI item most strongly associated with a fear response while running on the spot was "When I notice my heart is beating rapidly, I worry that I might have a heart attack." The ASI item most strongly associated with a fear response while spinning was "It scares me when I feel shaky." The ASI item most strongly associated with a fear response while hyperventilating was "It scares me when my heart beats rapidly" and "It scares me when I become short of breath."

Antony and colleagues' (2006) findings were consistent with those of Schmidt and Trakowski (2004). About two-thirds of the people with panic disorder responded with at least moderate fear to at least one of the symptom-induction exercises, and over a third responded with moderate fear to at least three of the exercises. One interesting finding was the tendency of people with panic disorder to report fear of one of the control exercises, "Imagining being in a peaceful place." People in the nonclinical control group didn't report similar fear. Though this finding was unexpected, it's consistent with previous research showing that some people with panic disorder experience fear during relaxation exercises (Adler, Craske, and Barlow 1987). Some exercises were fairly reliable in triggering fears (particularly, spinning, hyperventilation, breathing through a straw, and using a tongue depressor). These results are similar to those of Schmidt and Trakowski (2004), suggesting that these particular exercises might be best tried first with patients with panic disorder. Other exercises were less effective (particularly, putting the head between the legs and lifting quickly, staring at a light and then reading, tensing muscles, running on the spot, or sitting facing a heater). A relatively small number of patients responded with fear when running on the spot. It's possible that one minute was not sufficient to adequately induce feared sensations. The running component in our program is ten minutes.

The following table provides a few examples of commonly used interoceptive exercises that have been found to reliably trigger fear of anxiety (Antony et al. 2006; Wald, forthcoming). It also includes a description of how to do each exercise to bring on the feared sensations. Please note that to ensure safe participation in interoceptive exercise in our own program (for example, running), participants are not invited to take part in the program if they have a health condition that precludes aerobic exercise as assessed by the Physical Activity Readiness Questionnaire (PARQ; Shepherd, Cox, and Simper 1981). In particular, we do not invite people to participate if they have peripheral vascular disorder, hypertension, gastrointestinal disorder, neurological disorder, pulmonary disease, cardiac disease, arterial disease, diabetes, seizure disorder, or liver disease. Similarly, the described exercises may not be appropriate for everyone. If you have any of the previously mentioned disorders, please consult your health care provider before trying these exercises. However, it is important to emphasize that these exercises are commonly used and are perfectly safe for the very large majority of people.

Interoceptive Exercise	Symptoms Most Strongly Elicited
Head shaking ✦ Shake head from side to side for thirty seconds.	1. Dizziness or faintness 2. Pounding or racing heart 3. Breathlessness or smothering sensations
Spinning ✦ Spin around while standing for one minute, or spin in an office chair.	1. Dizziness or faintness 2. Pounding or racing heart 3. Breathlessness or smothering sensations
Hyperventilating ✦ Breathe deeply and quickly for one minute at a pace of about one breath every two seconds, as if blowing up a balloon.	1. Breathlessness or smothering sensations 2. Dizziness, faintness, feelings of detachment or unreality 3. Pounding or racing heart
Straw breathing ✦ Breathe through a narrow drinking straw for two minutes. Combine with running on the spot or stair climbing to evoke more intense sensations.	1. Breathlessness or smothering sensations 2. Pounding or racing heart 3. Choking
Running in place ✦ Run in place for two minutes. Lift your knees as high as you can to enhance the effect.	1. Pounding or racing heart 2. Breathlessness or smothering sensations 3. Chest pain or tightness
Tongue depressor ✦ Place a tongue depressor at back of tongue for thirty seconds.	1. Choking 2. Breathlessness or smothering sensations 3. Nausea or abdominal distress

USE INTEROCEPTIVE EXERCISES TO INDUCE AND RATE YOUR SYMPTOMS

Following are instructions for how to proceed with interoceptive exposure (IE) and symptom assessment. These instructions have been derived from various sources, including Antony and colleagues (2006), Wald (forthcoming), Lickel and colleagues (forthcoming), and Barlow and Craske (2007).

1. Begin with the exercise that seems most appropriate for bringing on your particular set of feared anxiety symptoms. For example, if you're particularly bothered by sensations of breathlessness or smothering, then you might want to start with hyperventilation or breathing through a straw.

2. After completing each exercise, fill in the following table. In the first column, write down the name of the exercise you did, and then in the second column, write down all the sensations you experienced. Using a scale of 0 to 10, with 0 meaning no anxiety and 10 meaning extreme anxiety, rate your peak level of anxiety while performing the exercise, and write the number in the third column. Using a scale of 0 to 10, with 0 meaning no similarity to real-life panic and 10 meaning exactly the same as real-life panic, rate how similar the induced sensations were to those you typically feel when anxious, and write the number in the last column.

Exercise	Sensations Experienced	Peak Level of Anxiety 0 (none) to 10 (extreme)	Degree of Similarity 0 (none) to 10 (exactly)

3. Review your ratings of anxiety for those exercises with some simi-
    larity to your real-life anxiety. Now, create your own exposure
    hierarchy (see the next table) by listing the exercises in order of
    least anxiety provoking to most anxiety provoking. To learn that the
    physical sensations associated with anxiety are not harmful and that
    you can manage these sensations effectively, you need to practice
    these exercises beginning with the least fearful (easiest to tolerate)
    IE exercise and progressing to the most fearful.

4. Jaye Wald (forthcoming) advises that before you do each exercise,
    identify a specific catastrophic belief about the potential negative
    consequences of the feared sensations associated with the exer-
    cise, as well as an alternative non-catastrophic prediction about the
    outcome. Rate the strength of both beliefs (on a scale from 0 to
    100%).

Exposure Hierarchy	Anticipated Sensations	Catastrophic Belief 0 to 100%	Non-Catastrophic Belief 0 to 100%

5. After each exercise, record the peak anxiety you experienced during the exercise and the strength of your two predictions, catastrophic (maladaptive) and non-catastrophic (adaptive). Repeat each exercise until your peak anxiety rating shows at least a 50 percent reduction from pre-exercise levels. This reduction should be maintained over three consecutive trials. Once this is achieved, you can proceed to the next exercise on the hierarchy.

Note: The main goal in doing exposure exercises is to learn new ways to respond to your own physiological sensations. To achieve this goal, it's important that you not try to escape or avoid the induced sensations (by distracting yourself or taking fewer and more shallow breaths during hyperventilation) while performing each exercise. Such avoidance strategies will diminish your chances of success in learning to confront feared bodily sensations.

In our own research, we employ running as an interoceptive exposure technique for helping anxiety-sensitive people. To begin, we have high-AS participants engage in a running exercise for ten minutes in a gymnasium. Running triggers some of the same physical sensations we experience when anxious, such as a pounding heart, breathlessness, and sweating. Moreover, running is considered by some to be a more real-to-life interoceptive exposure exercise than activities such as chair spinning and breathing through a straw (Otto 2007). Running is considered safe, and even advisable, for patients with panic disorder (O'Connor, Smith, and Morgan 2000). Nevertheless, to ensure safe participation in the running exercise, we screen potential participants with the Physical Activity Readiness Questionnaire (PARQ; Shepherd, Cox, and Simper 1981) to determine if they have a health condition that precludes aerobic exercise (such as certain cardiopulmonary medical conditions). During the running, participants are encouraged to identify the automatic thoughts and feelings triggered by the physical sensations. With time and practice, participants habituate to the physical sensations associated with arousal, and their AS diminishes.

If participants reported panicking in response to running, they were encouraged to relax in a comfortable area and calmly reassure themselves that the symptoms they were experiencing were completely natural and not harmful in any way. Participants were encouraged to remind themselves that these symptoms would be expected due to the nature of the running task that increases arousal. Participants were taught how to do diaphragmatic breathing (slowly breathing in through the nose and out through the mouth; see chapter 8), and it was emphasized that this controlled breathing technique normalizes anxiety. Participants were encouraged to remain seated for another five minutes after panic-symptom resolution to show themselves that the panic symptoms were under control, and the importance of trying the exercises again soon was stressed.

Participants in our research program are assigned exposure homework. Specifically, they are required to run for ten minutes on ten separate occasions over the next ten weeks. Following each running session, participants complete a self-report questionnaire that measures their responses to the arousal induction challenge. The measure assesses their affective reactions (such as nervousness), cognitive reactions (such as the feeling of losing control), and somatic reactions (such as breathlessness) to the running exercises. Recent research in our labs (Sabourin et al., forthcoming) found that affective and cognitive reactions to the running decreased over exposure trials in the high-AS participants but not in low-AS participants (who were low to begin with).

CHAPTER SUMMARY

In this chapter, we looked at how changing our behaviors can alter our experiences of anxiety. We discussed both adaptive and maladaptive ways of coping with anxiety. In particular, we examined the use of interoceptive exposure as a technique for modifying our behavioral responses to anxiety by facilitating habituation to the feared sensations. In this way, we effectively learn "to be in anxiety." Research shows that interoceptive exposure techniques can help treat various anxiety-related symptoms (Deacon, Lickel, and Abramowitz 2008) and disorders (Wald, forthcoming). Interoceptive exposure techniques that involve physical activity (such as running) may provide additional benefits. For example, aerobic exercise yields positive effects on conditions commonly coexisting with anxiety disorders, including depression, hypertension, migraine headaches, and respiratory illness (Smits et al. 2007). In the next chapter, we'll talk more about these potential added benefits of physical activity for anxiety and stress management.

Chapter 8

Change Your Lifestyle

Bad habits are like a comfortable bed,
easy to get into, but hard to get out of.

—Anonymous

In chapters 6 and 7, we looked at how changing the way we think and behave can positively affect our anxiety management. In the next two chapters, we'll cover how establishing healthy-lifestyle habits can help us manage our stress more effectively. We'll begin by reviewing what stress is exactly and how lifestyle factors interact with it. Then we'll go on to determine our motivation to adopt a healthier lifestyle and how to enhance our chances of succeeding at making changes. To better understand stress, we need to go back to the man who first introduced the concept of "stress" into the research literature and the popular lexicon, Hans Selye.

STRESS

No one can live without experiencing some degree of stress all the time. You may think that only serious disease or intensive physical or mental injury can cause stress. This is false. Crossing a busy intersection, exposure to a draft, or even sheer joy are enough to activate the body's stress-mechanism to some extent.

—Hans Selye

Physician and endocrinologist Hans Selye is regarded as the father of the modern concept of stress. Some even refer to him as "the Einstein of medicine." He was born in Vienna in 1907 but spent most of his life in Montreal, where he served as director of the Institute of Experimental Medicine and Surgery at the University of Montreal. As the previous quote suggests, Selye believed that most of life was "stressful." He argued that stress results whenever we're faced with external changes or demands. Thus, a variety of events can result in stress, including a noisy environment, an argument with our partner, loss of a job, going on vacation, and injury or illness. Selye's research led to his now-famous theory, the General Adaptation Syndrome (Selye 1946).

General Adaptation Syndrome

Selye's General Adaptation Syndrome (GAS) outlines three stages that we go through when exposed to a stressor. The first is the alarm stage or "fight-or-flight" response. The alarm stage is our immediate physical response to a surprise or a threat, in which the body prepares us for life-threatening situations. In doing so, the body redirects resources away from the digestive and immune systems to more immediate muscular and emotional needs. If we can't fight or flee, or lack adequate skills for effectively coping with the alarm, then this stage might be followed by a stage of resistance as we adapt to the stress. According to Selye (1955), adaptation is at its optimum in the resistance stage. Our immune system is fighting to keep up with the increasing demands and expectations of the body. This requires functioning at an abnormally high level, and eventually the "stress" begins to take its toll. This is the exhaustion stage. Selye compared the exhaustion stage to the aging process and suggested that the three stages of adaptation are like the major periods of life—infancy, adulthood, and senility—"telescoped into a short space in time" (1955, 627).

The alarm stage is the stage most relevant for people with high AS, because this is where intense anxiety and even panic are experienced. Progression through the stages, however, can explain why people sometimes experience panic attacks not when they perceive stress most acutely but after the stressors have diminished, such as when on vacation.

Selye recognized that stressors could be both positive and negative. In his own words, "Adopting the right attitude can convert a negative stress into a positive one." He divided stress into two subgroups, eustress and distress, the former referring to pleasurable stressors and the latter referring to unpleasant or dangerous stressors. Due to individual differences in stress reactions, the same stressor could be pleasurable to one person and distressful to another. Apparently, Selye was fond of citing the example of the frustrated businessman who was forced by his family to go on vacation when he had so much to do (Berczi 1994). Thus, a vacation that would be pleasurable for most was a negative and stressful experience for this frustrated businessman. Consider another example: often it seems that we have either too much time and too little work, or too little time and too much work!

Interestingly enough, research shows that daily hassles can be more stressful than major life events. A daily hassle is the proverbial "straw that breaks the camel's back." Indeed, when compared with major life events, daily hassles are found to better predict both psychological and physical problems (Kanner et al. 1981). Major sources of stress can include loss of a loved one, lack of employment, financial problems, serious injury or illness, marriage, pregnancy, and vacation (Holmes and Rahe 1967). Even winning a lottery can be stressful. Examples of daily hassles include minor health problems, traffic jams, housework, home repairs, and nosy neighbors (Kanner et al. 1981) as well as too many e-mails and text messages. Do any of these sound familiar to you? Do you seem to have more major sources of stress or more daily hassles? Which kinds of stressors seem to bother you more? Which threaten to break *your* camel's back?

Major Sources of Stress   Daily Hassles

_____   _____

_____   _____

_____   _____

_____   _____

_____   _____

Stress and Anxiety Sensitivity

The vulnerability-stress model provides one way of understanding the relationship between anxiety sensitivity and stress. Vulnerability-stress models suggest that specific types of mental health problems (such as anxiety and related disorders) arise from a combination of vulnerability factors in the context of life stress. AS is a known vulnerability or risk factor for panic-related psychopathology (Taylor 1999). Moreover, an abundance of research indicates that stressful life events (such as job loss, illness, or divorce) are associated with anxiety symptoms (Benjamin, Costello, and Warren 1990) and often precede the onset of panic disorder (Rapee, Litwin, and Barlow 1990; Roy-Byrne, Geraci, and Uhde 1986). Laboratory-based research has found that uncontrollable and/or unpredictable aversive events contribute to elevated levels of anxiety and fear (Sanderson, Rapee, and Barlow 1989; Zvolensky, Eifert, and Lejuez 2001). In a direct test of the vulnerability-stress model of anxiety proneness with 390 Russian participants, Michael Zvolensky and colleagues (2005) found that the combination of high AS, in particular, physical concerns related to AS, and exposure to aversive conditions (such as lack of basic necessities, financial hardship, sense of insecurity, social stressors, or family pressures) in the previous month significantly predicted both panic attacks and agoraphobic avoidance.

In 2007, Swiss researcher Noortje Vriends, in collaboration with colleagues in Germany and the Netherlands, published the results of a longitudinal study investigating factors affecting recovery from social phobia in a community sample of 91 young German women. At the eighteen-month follow-up, 64 percent of the women were at least partially recovered, and 36 percent showed full recovery from social phobia. Significant predictors of recovery included less AS and less stress (including fewer daily hassles).

Anxiety-related distress is a common problem for Native American adolescents and adults (Dick, Manson, and Beals 1993). Shari Ann Robinson (2005), from West Virginia University, examined the relationships among AS, culture-related anxiety (such as anxiety about integrating into the majority culture and/or fear of becoming too acculturated), and stress in a sample 150 Native Americans. Robinson found that high levels of AS and high culture-related anxiety influenced perceived stress, which was associated with an increase in psychological problems.

Robinson proposed that high AS causes an individual to view his or her life situations as more stressful. This latter point is very important. It tells us that targeting your AS level is more important than targeting your stress level. Your perception of stress will diminish as you reduce your AS. Keep this in mind as we review basic stress-management strategies.

MANAGING STRESS

Adaptation to our surroundings is one of the most important physiologic reactions in life; one might even go so far as to say that the capacity of adjustment to external stimuli is the most characteristic feature of live matter.

—Hans Selye

How much stress is too much stress? How do we know if we're stressed? Are you stressed?

Think about how you've felt over the past two weeks. Check off the symptoms below that apply to how you've felt over the past two weeks or perhaps longer:

_____ Sleep disturbance (too much, too little, non-restorative)

_____ Appetite disturbance (too much, too little)

_____ Smoking more

_____ Drinking more

_____ Increased irritability and frustration

_____ Easy to anger

_____ Chest pain

_____ Breathing problems (sighing a lot)

_____ Digestive problems

_____ Tension in neck and shoulders

_____ Headaches

_____ Fatigue or lethargy

_____ Feeling edgy or anxious

_____ Feeling sad or tearful

_____ Problems with attention, concentration, memory

_____ General aches and pains

Now review your responses and consider whether your stress symptoms have increased or decreased over time. If your stress level appears to be increasing or remaining high, then you might want to consider making some changes in your lifestyle to reduce your stress (see the next section). But remember Selye's wisdom, that no one can live without experiencing some degree of stress on a daily basis. Life is stressful. That's why we need to have skills for managing our stress effectively, and a good place to start is establishing healthy lifestyle habits.

HEALTHY HABITS

We first make our habits, and then our habits make us.

—John Dryden

Our bodies are vehicles similar to our cars, trucks, boats, and motorcycles. We know that vehicles require regular maintenance or they'll malfunction. For example, if we don't change or rotate our tires on a regular basis, our car could develop a shake (shimmy) or worse (the tires could rupture). If we don't change the oil on a regular basis, the motor won't function at an optimal level and may actually seize up. Most of us prefer to properly maintain our vehicles, because we don't want to incur the costs of hiring a mechanic every time something goes wrong. Interestingly, we're more apt to attend to maintaining our cars and trucks than our own bodies, the vehicles we live in 24/7, even though neglecting proper maintenance of our bodies comes at a much higher cost.

Our bodies don't come with a user's manual, but if they did, the following recommendations would ensure optimal performance:

✦ A vehicle works best when it has proper fuel: *nutrition.*

✦ A vehicle works best when it has good ventilation for clean air and cooling effects: *breathing*.

✦ A vehicle works best when operated regularly at a level that brings the motor up to its regular working temperature. For the human body, this means daily *exercise*, or at least four times a week, at a level that raises the heart rate.

✦ Vehicles also require a break from operation, or at least their drivers do: *rest and sleep*.

Before reading any further, consider the condition of your own vehicle, your own body. Would you pass inspection if you were required to undergo a maintenance assessment? Complete the following checklist by indicating whether or not you think the quality of each component is okay. If not okay, what changes would you recommend? Once you've completed the checklist, read on.

VEHICLE (BODY) MAINTENANCE CHECKLIST

Date: _____ Model year: _____

Item	O = Okay N = Not Okay	Recommended Changes
Nutrition		
Weight		
Breathing		
Exercise		

Relaxation		
Sleep		
Sense of humor		

Maintaining Your Vehicle: Nutrition

In 2005, the U.S. Departments of Health and Human Services (HHS) and Agriculture (USDA) issued the following advice to all Americans: reduce calorie consumption, make wiser food choices, and increase physical activity. This advice was contained in the sixth edition of *Dietary Guidelines for Americans*. The following nutritional recommendations are derived from those evidence-based guidelines, *Canada's Food Guide* (Health Canada 2007), and the health education sessions that we employ in our own research.

Balanced Diet	Sodium and Potassium
✦ Follow recommendations of USDA or *Canada's Food Guide*. ✦ Choose a *variety* of nutrient-dense foods and beverages that limit intake of fats, cholesterol, added sugars, salt, and alcohol.	✦ Consume less than 2,300 mg of sodium (approximately one teaspoon of salt) daily, and limit salt added in food preparation. ✦ Choose potassium-rich fruits and vegetables.

Food Groups Encouraged	Fats and Carbohydrates
✦ Include a variety of fruits, vegetables, and whole-grain products each day. Consume from all five vegetable subgroups (dark green, orange, legumes, starchy vegetables, and other vegetables) several times a week. ✦ At least half the grains should come from whole grains. ✦ Opt for fat-free or low-fat milk or equivalent milk products.	✦ Limit fat, cholesterol, and sugar intake. Preferred fat sources are fish, nuts, and vegetable oils containing polyunsaturated and monounsaturated fatty acids. Opt for lean, low-fat, or fat-free meats, poultry, dry beans, and milk or milk products.
Water	**Alcoholic Beverages**
✦ Eight glasses a day are recommended to break food down into nutrients, remove wastes and toxins, lubricate bone and muscles, and keep from overheating.	✦ If you drink alcohol, don't exceed one drink per day for women or two drinks per day for men. ✦ Certain individuals or groups should abstain completely (such as pregnant and lactating women, children and adolescents, those taking medications that interact with alcohol, and those who are unable to limit intake).

Weight Management	Physical Activity
✦ Balance calories consumed with those expended (calories in = calories out). ✦ Make small decreases in caloric intake and increase physical activity to prevent gradual weight gain over time.	✦ Take part in regular exercise and reduce sedentary activities. ✦ For optimal physical fitness, include cardiovascular conditioning, stretching exercises for flexibility, and resistance exercises or calisthenics for strength and endurance.

Maintaining Your Vehicle: Breathing

Smile, breathe, and go slowly.

—Thich Nhat Hanh

The act of breathing is performed primarily by the diaphragm. The diaphragm is a large dome-shaped muscle that separates the thoracic cavity from the abdominal cavity. The thoracic cavity is the area of the chest protected by the ribs wherein the heart and lungs reside. When we breathe in, the diaphragm contracts, creating a vacuum that sucks air into the lungs. When we breathe out, the diaphragm relaxes. As the lungs deflate, air gets pushed out similar to the way an inflated balloon deflates when released. Your abdominal muscles help move the diaphragm.

Breathing is intended to facilitate the exchange of gases: cells in the body need to get oxygen and get rid of carbon dioxide (the waste product of cells). The respiratory center in the brain sets the breathing rate according to carbon dioxide levels rather than oxygen levels. When we're under stress, our breathing patterns can change. For example, individuals in the throes of anxiety may take small, shallow breaths, using their shoulders rather than the diaphragm to move air in and out of the lungs. This type of breathing (hyperventilation) results in too much carbon dioxide being expelled and upsets the body's balance of gases. Sometimes people breathe into a paper bag to restore carbon dioxide levels. Hyperventilation can actually prolong feelings of anxiety by exacerbating physical symptoms of stress.

Breathing and Stress

Stress can influence our breathing in a couple of different ways. Short-term stress (such as arguing with your partner, preparing to give a speech, enduring a computer crash, or being cut off in traffic) tends to increase our breathing rate, potentially leading to *hyperventilation* (over-breathing). On the other hand, long-term, chronic stress (such as from dissatisfying job situations, unhealthy relationships, chronic health or financial problems, or chronic feelings of helplessness or lack of control) can lead to *inhibited breathing* (underbreathing, or not breathing deeply or frequently enough).

David Anderson and Margaret Chesney (2002) suggest that an inhibited breathing pattern may be a habit conditioned from assessing the world as a difficult or dangerous place. An inhibited breathing pattern may actually contribute to chronic elevated blood pressure. This could happen if chronic underbreathing maintained high concentrations of carbon dioxide in the blood. This could result in increased kidney retention of sodium, which could affect blood pressure by way of increased blood volume and cardiac output (Anderson and Chesney 2002). Apparently, an inhibited breathing pattern is more commonly seen in women than men, and the reason isn't clear. Researchers propose that women and men respond differently to stress, with men more likely than women to show fight-or-flight responses (Taylor et al. 2000). Moreover, research shows that the impact of stress on blood pressure and heart rate can differ between women and men. Gender-specific influences of hormones may play a role (Anderson and Chesney 2002).

HOW DO YOU KNOW IF YOU'RE BREATHING CORRECTLY?

1. First, find a place to sit comfortably.

2. Place one hand on your upper chest and the other hand on your abdomen.

3. Breathe normally for one minute.

4. Which hand moves more?

If you said the hand on your chest, chances are you're not breathing as effectively as you could or should. If you said the hand on your abdomen moved more, then you may be breathing effectively, although we encourage you to read on nonetheless. Moving the diaphragm requires the use of the lower abdominal muscles, so if your abdomen doesn't gently move in and out as you breathe, then you may not be breathing correctly. Abdominal breathing or diaphragmatic breathing is similar to the "belly breathing" that babies do when they're sleeping peacefully. To get the most out of our breaths (including releasing stress from our bodies; see the next section), we need to shift from upper-chest breathing to abdominal breathing. Other indicators that you could improve your breathing are if your shoulders tend to move toward your ears when you breathe and heavy sighing, as if you're unable to fill your lungs fully.

Diaphragmatic Breathing

Both hyperventilation and inhibited breathing patterns can be modified by practicing diaphragmatic breathing. Diaphragmatic breathing is intended to help you use your diaphragm correctly while breathing. You can practice diaphragmatic breathing while lying on your back or sitting comfortably in a chair. Breathe in slowly through your nose and push your stomach out as if inflating a balloon. Try to minimize any movement in your chest or shoulders. Breathe out slowly through pursed lips. As you breathe out, tighten your stomach muscles, letting them fall inward (deflate the balloon). You should practice every day until the new habit of breathing diaphragmatically is established. Then, it will be available to you when a stressful situation arises. This simple technique can slow and even stop the fight-or-flight response. Once the diaphragm is doing the work, you can sit quietly and enjoy the sensation of physical relaxation. With each breath, allow any tension in your body to slip away. Some people find that saying to themselves "Re-" on the inhale and "-lax" on the exhale enhances the experience.

Some anxiety-sensitive people may find that, at first, concentrating on their breath actually increases their anxiety and provokes hyperventilation. If this is the case, don't worry; just review the instructions and try again. For many people, this kind of anxiety reaction is short-lived and will diminish with practice of diaphragmatic breathing. However, if the difficulty persists, you might consider consulting a professional to help you establish the practice. Here are some of the reputed physiological benefits of diaphragmatic breathing:

✦ Lowered blood pressure and heart rate

✦ Reduced amounts of stress hormones

✦ Reduced lactic acid buildup in muscle tissue

✦ Balanced levels of oxygen and carbon dioxide in the blood

✦ Improved immune system functioning

✦ Feelings of calmness and well-being

✦ Increased physical energy

Maintaining Your Vehicle: Physical Activity

A substantial body of literature attests to the beneficial short-term and long-term effects of exercise on physical and psychological well-being. Research shows that regular physical activity is a salient factor in the prevention and rehabilitation of many disorders, including coronary artery disease, hypertension, diabetes, colonic neoplasm, and coronary obstructive pulmonary disease.

Studies show that accompanying the fitness gains from exercise are improvements in psychological conditions such as anxiety, depression, and other mood states. Other psychological benefits attributed to physical activity include enhanced mental performance and concentration; improved self-image; feelings of confidence and the perception of mastery; greater sleep quality; and a reduction in perceived feelings of anger, time urgency, and time pressure (Byrne and Byrne 1993; DiLorenzo et al. 1999).

More specifically, regular exercise is associated with an increase in endorphins (literally, *endogenous* plus *morphine*) in the central and peripheral nervous systems both during and after exercise (Harber and Sutton 1984). Endorphins produce the following effects: pain relief, stress reduction, immune system enhancement, postponement of the aging process (Salmon 2001), and positive effects on mood (Peluso and Guerra de Andrade 2005). Other body chemicals, such as epinephrine (adrenaline) and dopamine (part of the brain's motivation and reward system), also tend to increase during exercise and are associated with increased positive affect (Harte and Eifert 1995).

In chapter 7, we looked at running as one type of interoceptive exercise for reducing your sensitivity to anxiety-related sensations. Running is a rather novel interoceptive exposure technique (Smits et al. 2007; Watt et al. 2008). The rationale for using an aerobic exercise (such as running) as an interoceptive exposure technique is that many highly anxiety-sensitive people avoid activities that induce anxiety-related bodily sensations, such as physical exercise, coffee, or even sex. For example, one study of thirty-eight patients with panic disorder revealed that most avoided aerobic exercise (Broocks et al. 1997). One possible reason for this avoidance is that physical activity, such as running, produces many of the same physiological sensations associated with anxiety (such as elevated heart rate, respiration, and perspiration). Thus, it's not surprising that highly anxiety-sensitive people avoid such activities. Lachlan McWilliams and Gordon Asmundson (2001) examined the relationship between AS and self-reported use of two arousal-increasing substances (particularly, caffeine and nicotine) and exercise frequency in a sample of 256 university students (77 percent women). They found no association between AS and use of the two stimulants. They did, however, find that higher levels of AS (especially physical concerns associated with anxiety) were associated with lower levels of reported exercise frequency, at least among the men. Jasper Smits and Michael Zvolensky (2006) observed a similar finding among 39 individuals suffering from

DID YOU KNOW?

In the late nineteenth and early twentieth centuries, people believed that men and women breathed differently. This belief was based on the observation that men breathed "into the belly" (with the diaphragm and abdominal muscles), whereas women breathed shallowly into the upper chest and rib cage. The difference, of course, lay not in biology but in fashion. Women of the day wore corsets, which significantly restricted abdominal movement. Wearing corsets forced women to find alternative strategies for breathing that put them at risk for anxiety and even fainting. Unfortunately, it seems that women are still at risk for problem breathing. Women are more apt to reveal an "inhibited breathing pattern" (shallow breathing and frequent breath-holding) than men. This type of breathing is associated with chronic stress, anticipatory fear, and a reluctance to express anger. This inhibited breathing pattern resembles the "freeze" response; that is, the tendency among animals (including humans) to play dead when threatened by something they can't run from (the "flight" response) or successfully overpower (the "fight" response). Research shows that women are more likely than men to avoid conflict or disappointing others, and also to feel powerless in work and social situations. Consequently, women may be more apt to use the "freeze" response in reaction to stress. Unfortunately, this inhibited breathing pattern may reinforce feelings of overwhelm and powerlessness, and moreover, is associated with harmful health outcomes, such as chronic hypertension (McGonigal 2005).

panic disorder. The physically inactive individuals reported significantly higher levels of AS compared with those who reported engaging in exercise during leisure time.

Two studies conducted by one of the authors of this book produced similar results. In a study on 226 high-school boys and girls, Margo Watt, Tara MacDonald, and Marie-josée Lefaivre (2008) found that for girls, AS social concerns (particularly, concerns that showing anxiety would result in social rejection) were related to decreased frequency of physical activity. For the boys, AS physical and psychological concerns (particularly, concerns that experiencing anxiety would result in physical or mental health problems) were related to decreased frequency of physical activity. Another study with varsity athletes (126 males and 79 females), conducted by Margo Watt, Derek MacDonald, and Lou Bilek (2008), found that the athletes had significantly lower levels of AS than typically is found in nonathletic undergraduate students. The athletes also reported significantly fewer childhood experiences in which they learned to fear arousal-related sensations than other undergraduate samples.

Although these studies provide evidence for the relationship between elevated AS and exercise avoidance, they don't indicate the causal direction of the relationship or the mechanism by which this relationship might develop. For example, people with high AS might avoid exercise because they fear the physical sensations, or people who avoid exercise might be at increased risk to develop high AS. If people with high AS avoid exercise, they may deny themselves an important opportunity to reduce their fears of the physical sensations through interoceptive exposure. Moreover, avoiding aerobic exercise may actually increase their risk for panic disorder. Some researchers (such as Broocks et al. 1997) have proposed that reduced aerobic fitness might actually contribute to development of panic disorder. Japanese researchers Hisanobu Kaiya and colleagues (2005) suggest that chronic avoidance of physical exercise may cause reduced intake of oxygen and accumulation of lactate, which could increase a person's susceptibility to panic attacks. However, people with panic disorder might come to dislike and hence avoid physical exercise, which then contributes to reduced oxygen intake and accumulation of lactate, leading to further panic attacks (Kaiya et al. 2005).

The findings of these studies suggest a few important things. First, high-AS individuals may avoid physical exercise, thereby increasing their risk for both physical health problems (such as lack of fitness or being overweight) and psychological health problems (such as panic disorder). Another implication is that individuals with high AS may avoid using an important strategy for coping with stress, namely, physical activity. Physical activity is believed to yield both anti-anxiety and antidepressant benefits, and to offer protection from the effects of stress (Salmon

2001). For this reason, physical activity has been promoted as a treatment alternative and/or treatment adjunct for a variety of anxiety and mood disorders, including panic disorder (Atlantis et al. 2004; Broman-Fulks et al. 2004; Dunn, Trivedi, and O'Neal 2001; Penedo and Dahn 2005). Provided they've been scientifically tested to be effective, treatment alternatives are valuable when considering options for therapy-shy clients (such as adolescents). Indeed, physical activity may be a particularly attractive alternative to traditional treatments, such as psychotherapy or medication, for certain client populations (such as the elderly). Moreover, exercise as a primary or adjunct treatment for anxiety may provide a cheaper and more accessible (less stigmatized) option, with fewer negative side effects (Dratcu 2001).

European researchers Andreas Broocks and colleagues (1998) compared a ten-week program of regular aerobic exercise (running) to an active drug therapy and placebo-pill condition in forty-six patients suffering from panic disorder. The participants were assigned to one of the three conditions at random. The researchers found that, compared with a placebo, regular aerobic exercise brought significant clinical improvement, although the effects weren't as immediate as the drug treatment. Josh Broman-Fulks and his colleagues (2004) investigated the effects of high-intensity versus low-intensity aerobic exercise on levels of AS in a nonclinical sample of university students. Highly anxiety-sensitive students were randomly assigned to six sessions across two weeks of either high-intensity or low-intensity exercise on a treadmill. Both groups showed significant reduction in overall levels of AS one week after completion of the program. The high-intensity exercise group, however, showed a more rapid reduction in AS levels and a higher reduction in fear of anxiety-related physical sensations than the low-intensity exercise group.

The authors (Watt et al. 2008) also have found promising results regarding the role of physical activity in reducing AS. In our research, high- and low-AS young women were randomly assigned to either a brief cognitive behavioral treatment or a control condition. Everyone participated in three 1-hour sessions delivered in a small group format over three days. The treatment groups received education about AS and its relation to anxiety and panic. These participants were taught how to identify and modify ways of thinking that could worsen their anxiety. Participants in the treatment condition also participated in a 10-minute running activity and were assigned homework involving 10 minutes of running or brisk walking at least ten times over the next ten weeks, which was when they were scheduled to meet again with the researchers. (Note that prospective participants for this study were screened in advance for any health reasons, for example, lung or heart disease, that might've precluded their ability to participate in the running component.) Results of our study showed a significant decline in AS levels for the high-AS participants in the cognitive behavioral treatment condition. No similar decline in AS levels was found for participants in the control condition or for the low-AS participants (Watt, Birch, Stewart, and Bernier 2006).

How Much Exercise Do We Need?

Health Canada's *Physical Activity Guide* (2007) advises sixty minutes of light-intensity activities every day to stay healthy or improve your health. The time needed depends on the effort. As you progress to moderate-intensity activities, you can cut down to thirty minutes, four to five days a week. It's important to note, however, that you don't have to do the whole thirty minutes at once. Your thirty minutes could be made up of three ten-minute bursts of activity spread across the day. Also, the activity can be a "lifestyle activity" (for example, walking in the mall or taking the dog out), structured exercise, or sport, or a combination of all three. Again, it's not the activity per se but the time and intensity that counts.

+ **Light intensity** (sixty minutes a day): Strolling/light walking, dusting, light yard work such as gardening, stretching, yoga, volleyball

+ **Moderate intensity** (thirty to sixty minutes a day): Brisk walking, biking, heavy yard work such as raking leaves, swimming, dancing, water aerobics, stair climbing

+ **Vigorous intensity** (thirty minutes a day): Aerobics, running, speed skating or hockey, basketball, fast swimming, fast dancing, tennis, cycling

(Health Canada 2007)

LOW-INTENSITY EXERCISE

During a typical week, how many days do you do *low-intensity exercise* (for example, yoga, pilates, leisure walking, and so forth) for at least thirty minutes? You may include low-intensity physical activity performed as a mode of transportation (for example, a fifteen-minute leisurely walk to school).

0   1   2   3   4   5   6   7

What type of low-intensity exercise do you do?

_____

MODERATE-INTENSITY EXERCISE

During a typical week, how many days do you engage in *moderate-intensity exercise* (for example, brisk walking, skating, bike riding, swimming, playing outdoors, and so forth) for at least thirty minutes? You may include moderate physical activity performed as a mode of transportation (for example, a fifteen-minute brisk walk to school).

0   1   2   3   4   5   6   7

What type of moderate physical activity do you do?

_____

VIGOROUS-INTENSITY EXERCISE

During a typical week, how many days do you do *vigorous-intensity exercise* (for example, running, soccer, and so forth) for at least thirty minutes?

0   1   2   3   4   5   6   7

What type of vigorous-intensity exercise do you do?

_____

ORGANIZED SPORTS

During a typical week, how many days do you take part in organized sports at school or in your community (for example, exercise class, sports team, intramural sports, running clinics, and so forth) for at least thirty minutes?

0   1   2   3   4   5   6   7

What type of organized sports do you do?

_____

ACTIVE LIFESTYLE

What is your main mode of transportation? Please rate these options from 1 for most frequently used, 2 for next most frequently used, and so on. Please leave blank those options that don't apply to you at all.

_____ Motorized vehicle (such as a car, truck, or motorcycle)

_____ Public transportation

_____ Biking

_____ In-line skating/skateboarding

_____ Walking

_____ Other (please specify) _____

When given the choice, do you typically take an elevator or escalator, or use the stairs (check one)?

_____ Elevator or escalator   _____ Stairs

Maintaining Your Vehicle: Rest and Sleep

Sleep that knits up the ravelled sleave of care
The death of each day's life, sore labour's bath
Balm of hurt minds, great nature's second course,
Chief nourisher in life's feast.

—William Shakespeare

After eating well, practicing our breathing exercises, and exercising for sixty minutes, we deserve a rest. All animals require adequate rest and sleep each day to survive. The opossum needs eighteen hours a day, dogs and cats need ten to twelve, and the elephant needs only three or four hours. On average, most people need about seven hours of sleep a night to ensure optimal health and well-being. Why we need seven hours, or any hours for that matter, is less clear. Whereas eating supplies us with nutrients, and breathing supplies us with oxygen and the expulsion of carbon dioxide, the primary function of sleeping has remained somewhat elusive. Total sleep deprivation leads to death in rats. Moreover, the death due to sleep deprivation occurs ten to twenty days faster than if the rats had been totally deprived of food (Siegel 2003).

Jerome Siegel explored the question of why we sleep in an article for *Scientific American* in 2003. The key seems to be related to the function of rapid eye movement (REM) and non-REM sleep, and why we need both. During REM sleep, we experience our most vivid dreams and our brain activity resembles a waking state. During non-REM sleep, however, vivid dreams are rare, and our breathing and heart rates tend to be regular. Brain cells tend to fire in synchrony like an idling automobile, and according to Siegel, less energy is consumed when the brain "idles" this way. While we sleep, REM sleep alternates with non-REM sleep in a regular cycle. As we age, the portion of each day devoted to REM sleep declines. New research suggests that sleep is necessary for the following reasons:

✦ Reduced activity during non-REM sleep may give brain cells a chance to repair themselves.

✦ Interrupted release of neurotransmitters (such as serotonin, adrenaline, and histamine) during REM sleep may allow the brain's receptors for those chemicals to recover and regain full sensitivity, which helps regulate mood and learning.

✦ The intense neuronal activity of REM sleep in early life may allow the brain to develop properly.

Most adults have experienced sleeplessness at one time or another in their lives. General population surveys consistently find that roughly one-third of the American adult population report sleep problems (National Sleep Foundation 2005). Ten to fifteen percent experience clinically significant insomnia (Breslau et al. 1996; Ohayon 1996, 1997, 2002). According to the American Psychiatric Association (APA 2000), insomnia is characterized by problems in one or more of four sleep domains: difficulty getting to sleep, difficulty staying asleep, waking up very early in the morning, and not feeling rested even after ample time in bed (called *non-restorative sleep*). Insomnia affects all age groups, and its incidence increases with age. Among older adults, insomnia affects women more often than men. Stress can trigger short-term insomnia and may contribute to longer-term sleep problems.

Using data collected in the National Co-morbidity Study, Thomas Roth and colleagues (2006) at the Sleep Disorders Clinic in Detroit, Michigan, found that all four sleep problems were significantly higher in those with anxiety disorders. All four sleep problems were significantly related to role impairment (for example, reduced quantity and/or quality of work) even after controlling for co-occurring mental health disorders. This means that sleep problems themselves, not related problems, were responsible for the role impairments. Non-restorative sleep, in particular, was more strongly and consistently related to role impairment than were the three other sleep problems.

To ensure quality nighttime sleep and full daytime alertness, practice good sleep hygiene. *Good sleep hygiene*, like good dental hygiene, refers to the practices and habits we maintain that enhance our chances of getting a good night's sleep.

For good sleep hygiene:

✦ Maintain a regular sleep and wake routine seven days a week. Avoid napping during the day, or limit napping to thirty to forty-five minutes.

✦ Establish a relaxing pre-sleep ritual (such as a warm bath or a few minutes of reading).

✦ Avoid stimulants (such as caffeine, nicotine, alcohol, or spicy food) too close to bedtime.

✦ Regular exercise can promote good sleep, but avoid vigorous exercise before bed. Relaxing exercise, such as yoga or diaphragmatic breathing, can promote good sleep.

+ Make sure that your sleep environment is pleasant and relaxing, with a comfortable bed, pleasant room temperature, and relatively dim lighting. Avoid watching TV or listening to the radio in bed.

+ If you awaken during the night, don't "fight with the bedsheets." Get out of bed and leave the bedroom, read, have a light snack, do some quiet activity, or take a bath.

+ Don't take your worries to bed. Remind yourself that losing valuable sleep won't help your problems.

Some people with persistent sleep problems may need specific assistance from a health care professional.

Maintaining Your Vehicle: Humor

A good laugh and a long sleep are the best cures in the doctor's book.

—Irish Proverb

Of course, no discussion of healthy lifestyle would be complete without mentioning the importance of having a good dose of humor. "A joke is a very serious thing," according to Winston Churchill, and the research seems to support his contention. Indeed, the research evidence indicates that humor reduces the anxiety brought on by stress (Yovetich, Dale, and Hudak 1990). Making a joke about a stressful situation provides a sense of control over the stressor and a sense of connection with others (Henman 2001). A joke about a stressful situation (such as combat or the workplace) can render it less threatening. Humor makes people feel less afraid, because without fear they feel a greater sense of control (Dixon 1980), which is incompatible with feeling anxiety.

Recently, Hungarian researcher Attila Szabo (2007) compared the psychological effects of exercise to those of humor in a sample of twenty-four women. Results showed that watching an episode of the popular *Friends* TV series produced generally similar benefits on mood as exercise (particularly, cycling). Improvements in tension, negative mood, anger, and confusion were similar across both treatments. Fatigue and total mood disturbance were lower, and vigor and positive affect were higher thirty and ninety minutes after exercise. This suggests that the effects of exercise may last longer than the effects of humor. Researchers concluded that an episode of light-hearted humor could mimic some of the psychological benefits of exercise, but the duration of a number of positive changes are shorter than after exercise. It appears that comic relief is indeed time well wasted.

CHAPTER SUMMARY

There's a line in the Federico Fellini film *La Dolce Vita* that says, "I want to live my life so that it cannot be ruined by a phone call." In some ways, this statement captures the essence of why we should practice good stress management on a regular basis: so that no one event can completely derail us. As discussed in this chapter, good stress management depends on a healthy body. And a healthy body (like a vehicle) requires fuel, adequate ventilation, exercise, and regular maintenance. It's imperative to bear in mind, however, that stress is a part of real life. Given that we can't avoid stress, it's important to learn ways to better tolerate stress and manage it more effectively. Research tells us that an important way to better manage our stress is to turn down the amplifier by working on our AS. After reviewing the myriad benefits of reducing our AS and adopting habits for healthy living, we must decide whether we're prepared to make the changes that will ensure our health and well-being in the long term. Changing our behavior can be difficult, and it may be hard to know if we're ready to initiate behavioral changes. In the next chapter, we'll examine our motivation for adopting a healthier lifestyle.

Part IV

Preventing Relapse

Chapter 9

Establish and Extend Treatment Gains

Do your best every day, and your life will gradually expand into satisfying fullness.

—Horatio W. Dresser

In chapter 8, we looked at the role of a healthy lifestyle in helping us manage our anxiety and stress more effectively and over the longer term. In this chapter, we'll look at how you can determine what stage of change you're in with respect to initiating behavioral change. Thinking about changing our behavior (such as eating better, becoming more physically active, reducing our avoidance, or initiating interoceptive exposure exercises) can be daunting. On one hand, we want to change; on the other hand, we don't. Change means moving beyond the familiar, so it can be intimidating. In this chapter, we'll look at one technique that some people find helpful in making difficult decisions. We'll review techniques for initiating and managing change, and assess your personal confidence that you can affect change (that is, your sense of self-efficacy). Finally, we'll look at how to extend our new habits (such as reduced avoidance behavior and persistence in the face of anxiety) into the future. We begin, however, with the process of change.

CHANGE

Change is a process, not an endpoint. James Prochaska, Carlo DiClemente, and their colleagues recognized that when they developed their "transtheoretical model" of behavior change (Prochaska and DiClemente 1983; Prochaska, DiClemente, and Norcross 1992; Prochaska and Velicer 1997). The transtheoretical model uses a continuum of change readiness that suggests that people vary in the degree to which they're ready to engage in new adaptive behaviors. The transtheoretical model focuses on the individual's decision-making capacities. The model provides a template for the process of change.

The transtheoretical model has four dimensions: stages of change, decisional balance scale, processes of change, and self-efficacy.

Stages of Change

The transtheoretical model suggests that adopting a new behavior involves progression through a number of stages: (1) *pre-contemplation* (no intention to change behavior in next six months), (2) *contemplation* (intention to change within six months), (3) *preparation* (small or inconsistent changes), (4) *action* (active involvement in new behavior for less than six months), (5) *maintenance* (sustained behavior change for at least six months), and (6) *relapse* (resumption of old habits). No one stage is more important than the other, and progression through the stages isn't always linear. Indeed, people may make several attempts (that is, relapse phases) before reaching the maintenance stage. The transtheoretical model explains why simply telling a problem drinker to stop drinking is often futile and may even be counterproductive. If this person is still in the pre-contemplation stage, he or she isn't ready to change (Zimmerman, Olsen, and Bosworth 2000). Each person must decide for himself or herself when a stage is completed and when it's time to move on to the next stage. Stable, long-term change must come from within (internal motivation); it cannot be imposed from without (for example, due to pressures from a family member).

Since its development, the stages-of-change model has been applied to numerous problems. The model predicts outcome from smoking-cessation programs (DiClemente et al. 1991), pain-management therapies (Kerns and Rosenberg 2000), and weight-loss treatments (Ingledew, Markland, and Medley 1998), as well as other problem health-related behaviors (such as gambling, lack of condom use, difficulty adopting exercise, and so on). With regard to anxiety disorders, two studies of benzodiazepine treatment of panic disorder (Beitman et al. 1994 and Reid et al. 1996) found that participants at lower (versus higher) stages of readiness showed significantly fewer anxiety reductions. Similar findings have been reported with benzodiazepine response in generalized anxiety disorders (Wilson, Bell-Dolan, and Beitman 1997). These interesting findings show that a person's readiness to change his or her problematic behaviors can even impact responses to a biological treatment such as a medication.

While we don't normally think of anxiety as involving ambivalence to change (surely all anxious people desperately want to change!), Henny Westra and David Dozois (2008) argue that there's clear ambivalence. For example, a person with high AS may desperately want to be free of the fear of the anxiety sensations but lack the necessary motivation to engage in the interoceptive exposures needed to get past his or her AS. This is not too surprising given that exposure is the antithesis of the escape and avoidance behavior commonly seen in people with anxiety-related problems. The challenge then is to enhance motivation.

In 2004 Canadian researchers David Dozois, Henny Westra, Kerry Collins, Tak Fung, and Jennifer Garry assessed stages of change in a sample of eighty-one people with panic disorder. The stages of change were calculated at initial assessment and after a group treatment program involving cognitive behavioral therapy for anxiety management. Results showed that people who dropped out of the program had lower action scale scores than those who completed the program. High pre-contemplation scores and low contemplation scores were associated with reduced treatment outcome. Patients in the pre-contemplation stage were less likely to seek help for their anxiety, compared with patients in the stages of contemplation, action, and maintenance.

Stage of Change	Characteristics
1. Pre-contemplation	Not ready to initiate change. Not intending to take action in the next six months. For example, the person with high AS who can't imagine any other way of managing anxiety-related fears other than to avoid situations that trigger anxiety.
2. Contemplation	The person with high AS who needs to learn how to manage his or her anxiety-related fears better but doesn't know how and wonders at what cost. This person sees the barriers and benefits of change but is ambivalent about making changes. Intends to change in next six months but not considering change within the next month. It can be easy to get stuck in this stage.
3. Preparation	Getting ready to change. Planning to take action within the next month to better manage anxiety-related fears. May have done something already (such as read a book like this one or talked to a physician or mental health counselor). May attempt small modifications to behavior as determination to change increases (for example, approaching fear-inducing situations and trying not to procrastinate).
4. Action	Making change. Practicing new habits for the past three to six months. Example: Participating in a program designed to reduce AS. Enrolling in an aerobics class to establish a regular exercise routine.
5. Maintenance	Sustaining new habits for more than six months. Working to prevent relapse.

6. Relapse	Abandoning new habits to resume old habits. Most people "recycle" through the stages of change several times (relapsing) before change becomes truly established. Person should be encouraged to focus on success to date (versus failure) and to re-engage in change process. He or she should not heed Homer Simpson's advice (below).

Kids, you tried your best and you failed miserably.
The lesson is, never try.

—Homer Simpson

Hopefully, you don't agree with Homer Simpson's sentiment that you should never try, lest you fail. Research has shown that up to 80 percent of people aren't ready to go to the action stage right away. Change is something we have to work up to, and not everyone moves at the same pace. If we're not ready to take action, we'll resist pressure to change.

How can we tell if we're ready to make changes in our anxiety-sustaining behaviors? Are you ready to change your AS? Where are you in the stages of change? Consider the following questions and place a *Y* for yes, *N* for no, or *M* for maybe beside each one:

1. Do you think your anxiety-related fears are a problem for you?
    ____

2. Do you think your avoidance of anxiety-related situations is a problem for you? ____

3. Do you question whether your anxiety-related fears make sense?
    ____

4. Have you been thinking about making changes to reduce your anxiety-related fears (and avoidance behavior) in the next six months? _____

5. Have you been thinking about making changes to reduce your anxiety-related fears in the next thirty days? _____

6. Have you taken any steps to reduce your anxiety-related fears or avoidance behaviors in the past three to six months? _____

7. Have you been engaging in activities that expose you to your feared sensations (such as playing sports)? _____

8. Have you been engaging in activities that expose you to anxiety-related sensations and situations (such as public speaking) for more than six months? _____

9. Have you found yourself starting to avoid activities that provoke anxiety-related sensations (such as exercise) again? _____

10. Have you found yourself starting to avoid situations (such as social events) that provoke anxiety-related sensations again? _____

To determine your stage of change, compare these reponses to the previous stages-of-change table. For example, if you're a smoker and you responded no to the first three questions, then you're probably in the pre-contemplation stage. If you responded maybe, you're probably ambivalent about change. If you responded yes, then you're likely in the contemplation stage. If you responded yes to questions 4 and 5, then you're in the preparation stage. If you answered yes to questions 6 and 7, then you're in the action stage. If you answered yes to question 8, then you are in the maintenance stage. If you answered yes to 9 or 10, however, you may be relapsing.

If you're still in the pre-contemplation or contemplation stage, then it might help to use the decisional balance scale.

Decisional Balance Scale

Decision making can be difficult, especially when it comes to modifying well-ingrained and familiar habits, for example, avoiding anxiety-provoking situations, always distracting yourself from your anxiety-related sensations, or using drugs or alcohol to cope with your anxiety sensitivity. One thing people sometimes do to help themselves make decisions is to create a decisional balance scale. A *decisional balance scale* reflects the relative weighing of the *pros* (advantages) and *cons* (disadvantages) of continuing a current behavior (such as avoidance, distraction, or escape) or adopting a new behavior (such as learning to tolerate the sensations associated with anxiety). For most of us, before we're ready to change, the pros for changing must outweigh the cons. For example, people in the pre-contemplation stage typically see more reasons to maintain the status quo than to change. To move from pre-contemplation to contemplation, the person must come to see more advantages to reducing his or her AS levels and accompanying avoidance behavior than disadvantages (anticipating more fear by facing fears). To move from contemplation to preparation and action, there must be a decrease in cons. During the action and maintenance stages, the cons *must* decrease as the advantages of change become more prominent (Plotnikoff et al. 2001).

- ✦ What are the pros and cons of reducing AS?

- ✦ What are the advantages of the way things are now?

- ✦ What are the difficulties of doing things differently?

- ✦ What are the disadvantages of things right now?

- ✦ What would be the benefits of doing other things?

Following is an example of a decisional balance box intended to help someone decide whether to start doing more physical activity as part of his or her overall strategy for tackling AS.

Pros	Cons
Doing more physical activity would help me habituate to the physical sensations associated with the anxiety that I fear.	Doing more physical activity will expose me to the fearful physical sensations associated with anxiety. Something awful could happen.
Doing more physical activity would help me control my weight.	I don't have time to do more physical activity.
Doing more physical activity would be better for my health.	I don't like the way my body feels when I'm physically active. I don't like sweating and feeling tired.
Doing more physical activity would help me sleep better.	Doing more physical activity would mean less time for my family and friends.
Doing more physical activity would help me reduce tension or manage stress.	I don't like doing physical activity because I worry about looking awkward if others see me.
By doing more physical activity, I would set a good example for my children.	Doing more physical activity would cost too much money.

Create your own decisional balance box and examine your reasons for wanting (or not) to make necessary changes to reduce your AS. First, identify the cons of change (reasons for maintaining the status quo), and then identify the pros of change (reasons why reducing your AS levels may be desirable). Now rank the importance of your pros and cons by assigning each a weight, with 1 being slightly important, 2 moderately important, 3 very important, and 4 extremely important. Add up the weights. If the pros outweigh the cons, then it is time to consider making a change.

Pros	Cons

The processes of change are the strategies and techniques people use to change a problem behavior or adopt a new behavior. Research shows that people use different strategies at different stages of change (Prochaska and Velicer 1997). For example, in the earlier stages of change, people might increase their awareness by learning more about high anxiety sensitivity and its relation to anxiety disorders (such as panic disorder) and other disorders (such as depression). They might weigh the social consequences of their avoidance behavior (for example, reduced contact with friends) and they might consider accessing individual counseling or group-based programs (for example, brief cognitive behavioral therapy) designed to reduce anxiety sensitivity. As they transition into the later stages of change, they might monitor their avoidance behavior and push themselves to confront feared situations. They might enlist people who support their efforts to change their anxiety-related behavior and substitute healthy behaviors for problem behaviors (for example, exercising instead of using drugs or alcohol, or facing fears instead of avoiding them). Finally, they might reward themselves for progress made and further commit to change (Velicer et al. 1998).

SELF-EFFICACY

In order to change, we must believe that we can change. According to Albert Bandura (1994), perceived self-efficacy is our beliefs about our capabilities to produce designated levels of performance that influence events affecting our lives. Self-efficacy beliefs determine how we feel, think, self-motivate, and behave. In terms of the stages of change, self-efficacy reflects our confidence in our ability to engage in a specific behavior and resist temptation to relapse into old habits. Self-efficacy is less salient in the earlier stages but increases as we progress from precontemplation to maintenance. Self-efficacy remains high as the behavior is sustained (Marcus et al. 1994).

ASSESS YOUR SELF-EFFICACY

Imagine that you'd like to start practicing interoceptive-exposure exercises on a regular basis. How confident are you that you can continue with your routine under the following circumstances? Use the scale provided, and write in the number that corresponds to your level of confidence.

I	2	3	4	5

Not at all confident   *Extremely confident*

1. You're a little tired.   _____

2. You're in a bad mood.   _____

3. You're doing the exercises by yourself. _____

4. The exercises become boring. _____

5. You don't notice any improvements. _____

6. You have other demands. _____

7. You feel stiff or sore. _____

8. You have a bad day at work or school. _____

9. You go on vacation. _____

10. Others are making fun of you. _____

How did you score? How confident are you in your ability to incorporate interoceptive-exposure activities into your regular routine as a means of reducing your fears of bodily sensations? What other factors could get in the way of maintaining this new routine?

According to Albert Bandura (1994), there are four main sources of self-efficacy. (1) The first and most influential is personal experience with success in the past, or mastery experience. Outcomes interpreted as successful raise our self-efficacy; outcomes interpreted as failures lower our self-efficacy. Practicing your interoceptive-exposure exercises and noticing improvements in your response to anxiety will enhance your sense of self-efficacy. (2) The second source of self-efficacy is observing the effects produced by the actions of others, social models such as parents, peers, coaches, and teachers. Surrounding ourselves with competent social models transmits knowledge and teaches us effective skills and strategies for managing environmental demands; for example, watching and learning from someone who is lower in AS could help elevate our own self-efficacy about our ability to handle anxiety sensations. (3) Social persuasion or encouragement is a third way of developing self-efficacy. If others persuade us that we possess the capabilities to master given activities, we're more likely to mobilize and sustain greater effort. Thus, having a friend who encourages your desire to alter your response to anxiety can be very helpful for increasing your belief in your ability to make changes in your behavior.

(4) Physiological states such as anxiety, stress, arousal, and fatigue, as well as mood states, also impact self-efficacy, because people interpret

their symptoms of stress and tension as indicators of vulnerability to poor performance, and thus experience lower self-efficacy. People's moods also can affect their judgments of personal efficacy. A positive mood enhances perceived self-efficacy, whereas a negative mood diminishes it. According to Albert Bandura (1994), when people experience fears about their capabilities, these negative emotional reactions can further lower perceptions of capability, thereby triggering the stress and agitation that help ensure the inadequate performance they fear. This is similar to a self-fulfilling prophecy. Therefore, one way to modify people's self-efficacy is to reduce their stress responses, address their misinterpretations of physical states, and enhance their moods. So, reducing a person's AS should increase his or her sense of self-efficacy for managing and tolerating anxiety.

CHAPTER SUMMARY

In this chapter, we've examined ways of initiating, attaining, and maintaining behavioral change. The stages of change model provides a helpful template for assessing our motivation to modify problem behavior (such as avoidance of arousal sensations) and promote more adaptive behavior (such as engaging in activities to increase distress tolerance). Hopefully, you've learned some strategies for implementing and sustaining change. Now that you've modified your maladaptive behavior (for example, reduced your fears of anxiety sensations and avoidance behavior) and are maintaining new adaptive behavior (facing your fears), how do you extend these gains into the future? In the next chapter, we'll examine what you can do to stay on track.

PRE-CONTEMPLATION
Not ready to initiate change.

CONTEMPLATION
Seeing the barriers and benefits but feeling ambivalent about making changes.

PREPARATION
Getting ready to change.

ACTION
Making change. Practicing new behaviors for 3–6 months.

MAINTENANCE
Sustaining change. Practicing new behaviors for more than 6 months.

RELAPSE
Abandoning new habits to resume old habits.

But remember: if at first you don't succeed, try, try again.

Chapter 10

Preparing for Setbacks

Rather than viewing a brief relapse back to inactivity as a failure,
treat it as a challenge and try to get back on track as soon as possible.

—Jimmy Connors

In chapter 9, we looked at how to develop and maintain healthy lifestyle habits into the future. Implementing any kind of change takes time. As humans we tend to resist change. Moreover, it's easy to resume old habits, to lapse back into old routines. In fact, slipping back into old habits (lapses) is quite normal. The important thing is to keep from letting them turn into full-blown relapses. In this chapter, we'll examine what contributes to lapses and relapses. We'll look at how to reduce our risk of falling back into familiar ways of thinking and behaving, in other words, how to prevent "falling off the wagon" with respect to our attempts to overcome anxiety sensitivity.

PREVENTING RELAPSE

The word "relapse" derives from the Latin "to forswear," meaning to swear falsely, to repudiate under oath, to make oneself guilty of perjury. Typically, a *relapse* is defined as a series of recurrent lapses accompanied by a feeling of loss of control (Brownell et al. 1986). As it pertains to health, a relapse is a return of symptoms (signs, sensations, behaviors, thoughts, beliefs, and self-talk) associated with a maladaptive state (disease, disorder, or habit) after a period of relief from symptoms.

Relapse prevention refers to strategies or treatments applied in advance to prevent the reoccurrence of symptoms and/or the adverse condition. The components of a successful relapse prevention plan are derived largely from the substance-abuse (Marlatt 1985) and adult-depression (Overholser and Nasser 2000; Teasdale et al. 2000) literature. Today, relapse prevention strategies (for example, reviewing coping strategies, identifying relapse triggers, and anticipating future areas of concern) are an integral component of traditional cognitive behavioral therapy for most disorders.

AS and Relapse Prevention for Panic Attacks

Research shows that anxiety sensitivity can play a role in maintenance and relapse of anxiety symptoms. In 1995, Anke Ehlers conducted a prospective study to identify factors associated with the occurrence and maintenance of panic attacks one year after initial assessment. Participants included thirty-nine patients with current panic disorder, seventeen former panic patients, forty-six infrequent panickers, twenty-two patients with simple phobias, and forty-five controls. At one-year follow-up, most (92 percent) of the panic-disorder patients continued to experience panic attacks, and 41 percent of the former panic patients relapsed. No significant effects of treatments delivered in the community were found. Infrequent panickers tended to be more likely to develop panic disorder (15 percent) than controls (2 percent). For all participant groups, the maintenance and relapse of symptoms were most consistently linked with AS, overattentiveness to physical sensations, and avoidance behavior. Patients with simple phobias or healthy controls who experienced their first panic attacks during the follow-up year had shown higher AS at initial assessment than non-panickers. These findings fit with Ehlers's hypothesis that individual differences in interoception (that is, sensitivity to stimuli originating from inside the body, such as heartbeat) may be related to maintenance of panic attacks. Individuals with high cardiac awareness may be more likely to notice changes in their heart functions, such as acceleration or arrhythmias. According to Ehlers, because panic-disorder patients are more likely than other individuals to interpret these sensations as dangerous (Chambless and Gracely 1989), these sensations may trigger panic attacks. Even though some research indicates that anxiety-sensitive people have greater interoceptive awareness (Stewart, Buffett-Jerrott, and Kokoram 2001), Ehlers' study indicated that AS and heartbeat perception may have additive effects in maintaining panic disorder. Thus, effective relapse prevention for panic disorder should involve work at keeping both AS and interoceptive awareness within healthy limits.

AS and Relapse Prevention for Benzodiazepine Dependence

Relapse of panic disorder after discontinuation of benzodiazepine therapy is a common clinical problem (Pecknold et al. 1988). Studies conducted by Timothy Bruce and others in the early 1990s, however, found that initiating cognitive behavioral treatment prior to drug tapering and discontinuation significantly improved the chances that panic-disorder patients could successfully discontinue their medication (Bruce, Spiegel, and Hegel 1999). A subsequent study conducted by Bruce and colleagues (1999) and described in the same paper found similar success rates at two-year and five-year follow-ups. Of particular interest in the latter study was that AS was the only significant predictor of successful benzodiazepine taper among panic patients receiving cognitive behavioral treatment. Indeed, the smaller the reduction in anxiety sensitivity levels over the course of treatment, the more likely patients were to relapse and resume medication. This finding fits with the cognitive behavioral perspective that physical sensations (such as withdrawal symptoms that people sometimes experience when discontinuing long-term use of benzodiazepines) serve as triggers to those with high AS and precipitate the fear and avoidance that lead to relapse and recurrence of benzodiazepine use (Barlow 1988; Clark 1986). To the degree that patients' AS can be reduced during treatment, they should be less vulnerable to deterioration and the need to return to benzodiazepine treatment (Bruce, Spiegel, and Hegel 1999).

AS and Relapse Prevention for Smoking

Anxiety sensitivity is believed to be an important explanatory construct in early smoking relapse. In theory, smokers with high levels of AS should be vulnerable to early relapse, because they're highly sensitive to initial signals of negative affect and bodily sensations (Zvolensky, Schmidt, and Stewart 2003). Under this type of high-stress situation, wherein physical nicotine withdrawal sensations arise, high-AS smokers may respond to such aversive internal stimuli by relapsing to smoking at higher rates to relieve such distressful experiences. Case studies support this account (Zvolensky et al. 2003). In 2007, Michael Zvolensky and his colleagues investigated the relationship between AS levels and early smoking relapse among a sample of 130 young-adult daily smokers from Mexico City. Results indicated that anxiety-related physical concerns, in particular, were significantly associated with early lifetime smoking relapse over and above the effects of negative affectivity, cigarettes smoked per day, and alcohol consumption, as well as beyond psychological and social concerns (Zvolensky et al. 2007).

Research conducted in our own labs (Mullane et al. 2008) examined the relationship between AS and smoking cessation outcome in a group of 119 adult smokers who were attending a smoking cessation program. Results showed that high-AS smokers were at a significantly greater risk for relapse. Elevated levels of AS at treatment outset correlated significantly with high states of anxiety during the first week after smoking cessation. We concluded that screening for AS at the outset of smoking cessation treatment may provide useful information for assessing relapse risk. If you want to stop smoking, working on reducing your AS might help you be more successful at quitting smoking.

AS and Relapse Prevention for Other Substance Abuse

One of the current authors, Sherry Stewart, along with Matt Kushner (2001) proposed two mechanisms by which AS might contribute to increased risk for relapse to substance abuse. One possibility is that AS might interact with the experience of withdrawal symptoms or cravings, increasing potential for relapse. Similarities between withdrawal symptoms and anxiety symptoms (such as sweating or heart palpitations) underscore the possibility that high-AS people might fear drug-withdrawal symptoms just as they fear that anxiety-related bodily sensations would put them at increased risk of alcohol or drug relapse as a means of escaping from intolerable withdrawal symptoms.

Another possibility is that high AS increases relapse risk by intensifying withdrawal symptoms. As an arousal-accelerating factor (Reiss 1991), AS might not only increase the severity of anxiety symptoms but also the magnitude of withdrawal symptoms (such as palpitations or dizziness). A study by Kushner and colleagues (2001) tested this proposed model. As expected, AS was significantly related to the tendency to drink for the purpose of coping with negative affect. Results also showed that AS influenced coping-related drinking motives indirectly through its direct effect on anxiety symptoms. In other words, AS led to increased anxiety experiences, which in turn contributed to increased drinking to cope.

AS and Relapse Prevention in Exercise Programs

Research shows that lapses and relapses occur with some frequency in exercise programs. Given that people with high AS tend to avoid exercise, theoretically (no empirical data available) they would be even more apt to abandon exercise programs. This underlines the need to plan for relapse prevention when promoting exercise programs for these individuals.

James Sallis and colleagues (1990) examined the lifetime history of relapse from exercise in a community-based sample of 1,811 people who completed an extensive mail-based survey. Approximately 60 percent of participants reported no relapses, 20 percent reported one or two relapses (defined as three or more periods of non-exercise for longer than three months), and 20 percent reported three or more relapses. Relapse histories of current exercisers resembled those of non-exercisers. For both groups, the most commonly reported reason for relapse was injury. The cause of the relapse, rather than the number, seemed to influence the probability of later reinstatement of exercise.

In 2005, Barbara Stetson and others investigated the factors contributing to successful long-term exercise maintenance. Stetson examined relations among the characteristics of high-risk situations for abandoning exercise routines, components of relapse prevention relevant to exercise slips, and follow-up exercise outcomes in sixty-five long-term community exercisers. Results showed that the use of positive coping responses was associated with reduced likelihood of slipping back into more sedentary habits. Positive coping responses included use of positive reappraisal (for example, "I reminded myself that I've had some of my best runs when I didn't feel like it") and task or problem solving (for example, "I decided to drive toward the gym, and I told myself I didn't have to exercise that long").

Whereas relapse prevention can be an important consideration in developing an exercise program, most relevant to our present purpose is that exercise can decrease the probability of relapse for AS reduction and other behavioral change programs. For example, studies show that exercise in conjunction with inpatient treatment for alcohol abuse is associated with significantly lower alcohol cravings (Ermalinski et al. 1997). Exercise as adjunctive treatment for alcohol rehabilitation also has been associated with lower levels of anxiety and depression (Palmer, Vacc, and Epstein 1988). Sinyor and colleagues (1983) found that follow-up abstinence rates were significantly higher among alcoholics who participated in a fitness program in conjunction with treatment for alcohol abuse, compared with alcoholics in a regular alcohol-abuse treatment program (Stathopoulou et al. 2006).

RELAPSE PREVENTION MODEL

In 1985, Alan Marlatt proposed a cognitive behavioral model of relapse prevention. Marlatt's model was based on data he collected from seventy male alcoholics. According to Marlatt's model, the relapse process is a function of high-risk situations and the person's response to those situations. If the person lacks effective coping strategies or confidence to deal with the situation (self-efficacy; Bandura 1977), then he or she is apt to resume old habits. As mentioned, initial setbacks or lapses aren't unusual when people are trying to change problematic behaviors. To prevent a lapse from turning into a relapse, we need to treat the lapse as a learning experience, an opportunity to hone our skills so that we don't lapse again. For example, finding yourself feeling anxious after you've largely overcome your fears is normal. In fact, researchers even have a name for this; they call it "return of fear" (Rachman 1989). It simply tells you that you need to continue practicing your exposure exercises and cognitive restructuring.

According to Marlatt's model, a relapse is a series of lapses or a return to the previous problematic behavior pattern, and a *prolapse* refers to getting back on track in the direction of positive change (Witkiewitz and Marlatt 2004). Whereas Marlatt's model was originally designed to teach people a wide range of cognitive and behavioral coping skills to avoid or deal with lapses or relapses to substance use, the model is not limited to substance abuse. Its principles are applicable to other conditions where behavior modification is desired, such as managing your AS and stress levels and maintaining positive health-related behaviors (such as diet, exercise, and sleep).

According to Marlatt and Donovan (2005), our risk for resuming a problematic behavior is a function of our ability to manage high-risk situations. High-risk situations include certain people, places, emotions, and thoughts that lead toward a lapse or relapse. Other factors, such as destructive thinking patterns, a lack of planning, and lifestyle imbalance, can influence our chances of success.

RELAPSE PREVENTION AND RETURN OF FEAR

Stanley Rachman (1989) developed the concept of "return of fear" to describe the reappearance of fear after exposure treatment. Research has found that the return of fear can be influenced by individual differences (such as initial level of fear), treatment variables (such as the speed of fear reduction and the order of exposure material), and post-treatment factors (such as experience with a stressful life event; Vansteenwegen et al. 2006). Some evidence also indicates that one's internal context (state of arousal) can influence the return of fear (Mystkowski et al. 2003). These findings suggest that, to minimize the likelihood of the return of fear, it may be beneficial to conduct exposure therapy in a variety of contexts, both internal and external.

WHAT ARE YOUR HIGH-RISK SITUATIONS FOR RELAPSE?

In light of what you've read so far, what do you think could contribute to your resuming old patterns of behavior? For example, if after reading chapter 6 you learned to challenge your thinking (particularly, overestimating the probability of a negative outcome and catastrophizing) to reduce your fear of anxiety-related sensations, what do you need to do to maintain this skill? If, after reading chapters 7 and 8, you initiated behavior and lifestyle changes (for example, eating better and exercising more), what could sabotage your success to date? For the sake of illustration, let's assume that you've started a new exercise routine. Let's examine your risk of relapsing into old patterns of exercise avoidance. You now do a thirty-minute walk, four times a week, and attend a water aerobics class at the local pool every Saturday morning. In the spaces below, list your high-risk situations—people, places, emotions, and thoughts that might elevate your risk of relapsing into exercise avoidance.

1. _____

2. _____

3. _____

4. _____

5. _____

Now, let's look for high-risk situations for more-general fear of anxiety and avoidance behavior. Experts in the area of relapse prevention (Marlatt and Donovan 2005; Witkiewitz and Marlatt 2004) have identified the following triggers for relapse. We've adapted these to make them more relevant to AS. See how these compare to your identified risk factors for slipping back into old habits (such as catastrophizing and avoidance).

Triggers for Relapse

Adversity

Examples: Adversity as it pertains to an exercise program could include bad weather, inconvenient time of day, being alone, negative emotions, and fatigue.

Suggestion: List situations where you may be tempted to stop your regular activity, if only for a few days (such as when on vacation, enduring a bout of flu, and dealing with demands of work and family).

Negative emotional states

Examples: Feeling sorry for yourself, failing to take responsibility for choices, externalizing blame, and being impatient about progress. Things aren't happening fast enough for you. You feel overconfident or believe you've conquered your fears forever.

Suggestions: Practice breathing and relaxation techniques, and remind yourself that change takes time, that "slow and steady wins the race." Plan and prepare for relapse.

Negative physical states

Examples: Overtired or following an unhealthy diet.

Suggestions: Monitor your fatigue level. Make sure you're getting enough sleep and following a healthy diet.

Negative thinking styles

Example: Cognitive distortions (see the next section).

Suggestion: Read *The Feeling Good Handbook* by D. Burns (see the resources section).

Social pressure

Example: Being teased by others for adopting new habits or behaving differently.

Suggestions: Practice what you'll say to friends or others if they don't understand or support your behavior change. Remind yourself of why you have initiated behavior change.

Lack of	*Example:* Telling yourself that you can't change, that
self-efficacy	being anxious is just the way you are, or that avoiding
	works just fine.

Suggestion:	Remember that each experience you have in
	successfully managing your anxiety-related fears will
	contribute to a heightened sense of self-efficacy.
	Self-efficacy is like a seed that needs to be nurtured
	to grow—and success is the fertilizer.

Cognitive Distortions

According to Aaron Beck (1976), *cognitive distortions* are errors in logic that commonly operate in various disorders, including anxiety and depression. Cognitive distortions can lead people to draw erroneous conclusions even if their perceptions of a situation are accurate. If their perceptions of the situation are erroneous, cognitive distortions can amplify the impact of the misperceptions. Catastrophizing and overestimating probability are two types of cognitive distortions discussed in chapter 6.

To illustrate how cognitive distortions can operate, consider the example of Clara. Clara tends to see things as either-or, or black-and-white. She views others as being all good or all bad. This type of distortion is referred to as *dichotomous* or all-or-nothing thinking. Unfortunately for Clara, this type of thinking leads her to draw conclusions that cause her unnecessary distress. For example, if her boss is not *always* kind and considerate toward her, then Clara perceives her as uncaring and even hostile. Of course, this upsets Clara, and she tends to waste a lot of energy and time in states of distress that she could avoid if she knew how to challenge her cognitive distortions (for example, examining the evidence; Burns 1989; Freeman et al. 1990).

Here are a few of the cognitive distortions that could constitute high-risk situations for relapsing into fears of anxiety and avoidance behavior:

All-or-nothing thinking: You see things in black-and-white categories. If your performance falls short of perfect, you see yourself as a total failure. "I slipped and had a cigarette; I might as well smoke the whole pack now." "If I don't have enough time to go to the gym today, I might as well not exercise at all." "I skipped class today because I didn't want to do my oral presentation; now I'm right back to where I started with not being able to manage my anxiety."

Disqualifying the positive: You reject positive experiences by insisting they "don't count" for some reason or another. You maintain a negative belief that's contradicted by your everyday experiences. "Sure, I spoke out in class last week, which was pretty courageous for me, but I skipped class to avoid doing the oral presentation, so I'm right back where I started."

Magnification (catastrophizing) or minimization: You magnify the barriers to adopting a new routine and minimize your achievements to date. "I can't exercise much, because my heart races too fast and I'm afraid it'll wear out." "Walking doesn't really count as exercise."

Should-statements: The "tyranny of the shoulds"—you try to motivate yourself with "shoulds" and "shouldn'ts," and "musts" and "oughts" as if you needed to be whipped and punished before you could be expected to do anything. You end up feeling guilty because you can't meet your own high standards, and disappointed and frustrated because others can't meet your standards either. This way of thinking tends to feed anxiety because we learn to anticipate failure, which undermines our self-efficacy. "I should go to that anxiety management program, because others expect me to go."

Mind reading: You assume that others are evaluating you negatively without evidence that this is the case. "My classmates must think I'm an idiot when they see my hands shaking and hear my squeaky voice."

Fortune-telling: You react to situations as if your expectations were facts. "There's no sense in my applying for that job, because I won't get it. Either I won't show up for the interview or I'll be so anxious during the interview that they won't hire me."

For more information on these cognitive distortions, see Judith Beck's book *Cognitive Therapy: Basics and Beyond* (1995). Now that we have examined the high-risk situations and triggers for relapsing from behavior change, let's look at relapse prevention strategies for managing anxiety, including fears associated with anxiety-related sensations. Some of these suggestions derive from the work of Marlatt and Gordon (1985), others have been gleaned from the Centre for Addiction and Mental Health (2007), and others from our own clinical practice.

What to Do to Prevent Relapse of Anxiety

Become an expert on your anxiety. Know your symptoms and learn to recognize when symptoms begin. Access resources such as books, videos, support groups, and reliable Internet sites (CAMH 2007). See the resources section at the end of this book for websites and sources of further information.

Identify high-risk situations. Plan and prepare for situations that elevate your anxiety (Marlatt and Gordon 1985).

Identify early-warning signs. Take note of disturbances in sleep, increased muscle tension, tendency to ruminate, and increased avoidance behavior. Review your sleep hygiene, practice diaphragmatic breathing and strategies for relaxing, and challenge your thinking. Continue to expose yourself to situations you associate with anxiety (Marlatt and Gordon 1985).

Anticipate and prepare for lapse or relapse. "Practice" a lapse or relapse. Imagine what it would be like to resume your former ways of dealing with anxiety. Imagine what you will do if you find yourself slipping back into old habits of thinking and behaving (Marlatt and Gordon 1985).

Cope with feeling overwhelmed. Stress, fatigue, and feeling out of control can trigger symptoms of anxiety. Practice being "in the moment." If a runner focuses too far down the road when running, he or she will become overwhelmed by the distance and stop running. Breathe and relax using diaphragmatic breathing. Yoga and mindfulness meditation can help you focus your mind on the here and now so you can "ride through" uncomfortable bouts of anxiety (CAMH 2007).

Expand your toolbox of coping skills (see chapter 11 summary). Practice positive self-talk. Engage in pleasurable activities. Explore new ways of nurturing yourself (CAMH 2007).

Enhance your self-efficacy. Practice your skills and notice what you're doing right. Celebrate your successes, no matter how small they seem to be. Be good to yourself. Winston Churchill maintained that courage was going from failure to failure without losing enthusiasm. Don't lose your enthusiasm. Do something! Take action. Learn something new: take a course, try a new sport, join a club, or plant a seed (CAMH 2007).

Enlist the help of others, or mentor others. Develop a social support network. Family and friends can help you recognize when stressful situations might trigger anxiety symptoms, and remind you of your skills when you feel discouraged (enhance your self-efficacy). Consider what you would say to someone else if he or she lapsed into old ways of behaving (CAMH 2007).

Keep your commitment. Review your plan for managing your anxiety and recommit to it. Remind yourself why you want to make this commitment. Stick to it (CAMH 2007).

Do all things in moderation. Strive for balance in your life (CAMH 2007). See the next table.

Moderation is not a new concept. Confucius, Buddha, and Aristotle all advocated the benefits derived from achieving a proper balance in life (Lugenbehl 2000). According to Aristotle, "Too much exercise destroys strength as much as too little, and in the same way, too much or too little food or drink destroys the health while the proportionate amount increases and preserves it." Good health and well-being, so it goes, resides somewhere between the two extremes of excess (too much) and deficiency (too little). The notion of striking a balance between two opposing poles may not apply to all situations (such as when decisive action is required). As it pertains to health, however, its application does seem appropriate more often than not. For example, there's some evidence that moderate levels of AS, as opposed to low, may be optimal for our functioning. Some researchers have suggested that the relationship between AS and abnormal functioning may be a curvilinear one, meaning that a moderate amount of AS may be more optimal than having either high or low AS (Cox, Borger, and Enns 1999).

A study conducted by Shostak and Peterson (1990) examined the performance of people with low, moderate, and high levels of AS on an anxiety-producing task (mental arithmetic). They found that the people with low AS appeared to behave differently than the others. More specifically, compared to people with moderate and high levels of AS, the low-AS group revealed an indifference to their own physiological arousal. This led Shostak and Peterson (1990) to suggest that low AS may be related to antisocial personality traits. Scott Lilienfeld and Suzanne Penna (2001) found a significant relationship between low AS and the callous, unemotional traits associated with psychopathy, a personality disorder characterized by antisocial behavior.

Consistent with these findings, a recent study by Joshua Broman-Fulks and colleagues (2007) found that AS levels were inversely related to retaliatory aggression. More specifically, community volunteers with lower AS levels were more apt to demonstrate extreme aggressive responses in a laboratory task designed to assess aggressive behavior. It seems that finding arousal somewhat aversive isn't such a bad thing. Experiencing physiological arousal as either too aversive (high AS) or not aversive enough (low AS) can get us into trouble. Diminished reactivity to anxiety and environmental stressors might contribute to an antisocial lifestyle, a lifestyle that many of us avoid because we fear the inherent risks (for example, jail). Thus, with this training program, we're not advocating for you to completely eliminate your AS. Instead, it's in your best interest to bring it into the moderate range.

THE GOLDEN MEAN

Here we've outlined some of the main indicators of health and well-being. Where are you on the continuum? How close are you to the golden mean? Use a scale of 1 to 5, with 1 meaning too much, 5 meaning too little, and 3 being the golden mean. Examples are given of the extremes of too much and too little.

	Too Much (1)	Where Are You? (1 to 5)	Too Little (5)
Sun	Sunburn, accelerated aging, and increased risk of skin cancer		Vitamin D deficiency and increased risk of such diseases as breast, colon, and prostate cancer
Exercise	Excess weight loss, compromising physical integrity, exhaustion		Deconditioning, obesity, increased risk for chronic pain
Food Intake	Obesity		Anorexia
Sleep	Depression		Insomnia
Breathing	Overbreathing (hyperventilation)		Underbreathing (inhibited breathing pattern)
Blood Pressure	Hypertension		Faintness, or syncope
Anxiety Sensitivity	Increased risk of anxiety and related disorders		Possible risk for other psychopathology (antisocial behavior)

We'll conclude this chapter on a hopeful note by looking at a theory suggesting that a bonus feature of cognitive behavioral therapy is its capacity to instill clients with hope. Moreover, this element of hope may account for cognitive behavioral treatment's ability to prevent relapse.

RELAPSE PREVENTION AND HOPE

In an article published in 2000, Rick Snyder and colleagues discuss the role of hope in cognitive behavioral therapies. According to hope theory, purposeful movement toward a given goal requires that the person perceive a way or means of achieving the goal and an ability (agency) to do so (Snyder, Irving, and Anderson 1991). In other words, one must both know the way and have the wherewithal to get there. According to Snyder, because hope theory is about goal attainment, it also predicts those facets of psychotherapy that should help facilitate relapse prevention. For example, if a client successfully treated for social phobia encounters a particularly stressful situation, it could trigger crippling anxiety. According to hope theory, the anxiety becomes a potential obstacle to the goal of maintaining skills learned in therapy. Cognitive behavioral interventions, however, are well suited to generating hope for clients in psychotherapy because of the strong emphases placed upon goal setting, strategy generation (for example, homework assignments), and modification of negative beliefs regarding goal attainment (for example, cognitive restructuring or interoceptive exposure). Snyder suggests it's the hope-inducing properties of such therapies that account, at least in part, for the efficacy of many cognitive behavioral treatments in preventing relapse in the longer term.

CHAPTER SUMMARY

In this chapter, we looked at how to establish and extend the gains we've made thus far, as well as how to plan for and perhaps even prevent both minor lapses and full-blown relapses into old ways of thinking and behaving. We examined how we can reduce our risk of falling back into familiar ways of thinking and behaving, in other words, how to prevent "falling off the wagon" with respect to our efforts to overcome anxiety sensitivity.

Chapter 11

Staying the Course

I'm not afraid of storms, for I'm learning how to sail my ship.

—Louisa May Alcott

We've reached the final chapter. It seems appropriate to end the book with the story of how someone was able to use the cognitive behavioral techniques described in this book to not only deal with her anxiety sensitivity but also to overcome a related, crippling full-blown anxiety disorder. To protect the confidentiality of people we've worked with clinically, Colette's story is actually a composite of several people's stories, all of whom wanted to share what they've learned about managing the fear of fear. We think the story illustrates well the challenges of living with the fear of anxiety sensations and resultant anxiety-related problems, fear that can interfere with functioning and threaten an individual's mental and physical well-being.

Case Vignette: Colette

I'm a twenty-two-year-old undergraduate at a small northeastern university. Two years ago, I was diagnosed as having social phobia, also referred to as social anxiety disorder. Let me tell you, finding out I had a certifiable disorder was a relief. Prior to that, I thought I was going crazy and going there alone. Discovering that my ways of thinking, feeling, and behaving had a name indicated that there must be others like me. It also meant that there was something I could do to feel better. Here's my story.

Looking back, I don't see myself as having been particularly anxious growing up, certainly not as a child. When I discuss this with my mother, however, she claims that there were definite signs very early on. Apparently, I was one of those babies who couldn't be soothed unless someone, preferably my mother, rocked me. She claims we went through two rocking chairs and many, many late-night drives together. I recall having been a somewhat shy child who preferred to play alone or with one or two close friends only. According to my mother, having too many people around seemed to overwhelm me. She vividly describes my distress at starting school at age five. For the first two months, she had to accompany me to school and wait outside for ten minutes, lest I escaped in tears. If I remember correctly, she shed a few tears too. My mother also recalls how I begged out of my ninth-grade class trip to Quebec at the very last minute. I remember deciding not to go because I simply wasn't interested, but my mother recalls it differently. She claims that I didn't want to go because neither of my close friends was going and I was uncomfortable with staying with other people in a hotel for five days.

Although no one in my immediate family has ever been diagnosed with an anxiety disorder, I think it's very likely that my uncle suffers from one. In fact, I'm pretty sure he has social anxiety disorder, just like me. I always just thought of him as being really quiet and shy. He only ever had one girlfriend. They ended up getting married, which was fortunate for him because otherwise he wouldn't use the phone. His wife makes all his phone calls for him. My mom tells me that my uncle refused to have a normal-sized wedding but instead insisted on inviting his parents only. He bought the property next to his parents' home and built his house there. When we visit him, he talks little except to my father (his brother) and grandmother (his mother). When my uncle has to talk to anyone else, he avoids eye contact and appears very uncomfortable. As my mother tells it, when she first started dating my father, my uncle never talked to or even looked at her. When she went to their place for supper, apparently his parents joked about his eating so quickly and then heading back to his room. Perhaps not coincidentally, my uncle works in the woods by himself, away from other people. My father's relatives lead simple lives, so I doubt if they view my uncle's behavior as anything but being reserved and private. Certainly, he has never been assessed for an anxiety disorder. But I'd wager a bet that, if he ever was assessed, he'd be diagnosed with full-blown social anxiety disorder.

When I think back, I don't recall any particular learning experiences that would've contributed to my developing social anxiety. Although my father tended to be quieter and more reserved than my mother, he was far more outgoing than his brother (my uncle). My mother was a pretty typical mother, I guess. She seemed to worry about us—my brother and me—more than my father did, and a lot more than we thought she needed to. I do know that an important part of what kept me sane throughout my elementary and junior high-school years was the fact that I was a good athlete. I lived and breathed soccer and was lucky enough to play on some fairly competitive teams. Academically, I did well too (at least in junior high school), although I did tend to procrastinate at times, especially when faced with a looming deadline. This tendency proved almost my undoing in university.

I succeeded academically, athletically, and socially throughout junior high school, but when I moved to a new school after tenth grade, I began to experience what I now know as social anxiety. Through soccer and a somewhat quirky sense of humor, I was able to make friends but, despite this, I often felt very alone and left out. I avoided most social activities, because my growing social anxiety limited my ability to socialize and interact with my peers. I became increasingly depressed, which only served to further increase my anxiety, because I feared that others would see through my mask of happiness, see my pain and anxiety, and judge me negatively. My low mood was accompanied by a growing apprehension about my health as well. In particular, I grew increasingly fearful about what I thought were unusual bodily sensations. For example, whenever I exerted myself physically I seemed to sweat a lot and struggle for a good breath, and my heart would race and sometimes flutter. I began to worry that there was something physically wrong with me. This combination of low mood and growing physical discomfort led to my abandoning participation in athletics toward the end of high school.

Despite the adverse effect my growing social anxiety had on my grades, I managed to get accepted to several universities. I knew my anxiety would be problematic in my new environment, but I never imagined the crippling severity it would eventually reach. Because of my growing discomfort around other people, I requested a single room on campus. In retrospect, not having a roommate was a big mistake, of course. Typically, a roommate is the first friend you make on campus. Whereas most people in my dorm attended freshman activities with their roommates and met people that way, I was forced to go by myself. I remember feelings of paranoia, as if everyone were *watching me and wondering why I was by myself. I came to believe that other people saw me alone and assumed that I was a loser or thought I was strange. If I heard laughter, I immediately assumed it was at my expense, that I must've done something stupid or somehow looked foolish. If for some reason I arrived at the classroom after class had started, I'd have to miss that day's class since I couldn't bear the scrutiny of the other students if I were to enter late.*

Before long I essentially stopped trying to make friends, because I thought it easier to be alone than to have the constant fear of judgment hanging over me. I stopped attending classes, because sitting alone was too embarrassing. The mere act of leaving my dorm room and seeing people from my floor was too stressful. I remember thinking, These people don't like me, because I avoid socializing with them; they must think I'm stuck up or weird. *I always assumed the worst when it came to others' perceptions of me. When someone did initiate a conversation with me, it was awkward. I couldn't make eye contact, my hands shook, and my voice often trembled. My mind raced trying to think of what to say next to avoid saying anything that could be perceived as stupid. Of course, this behavior just made these interactions worse, because I was sure that others could see my anxiety and judge me negatively.*

It was during these times that I first began to experience the wide range of physiological symptoms associated with anxiety. I always felt flushed, and my face sweated profusely. My chest always felt tight, and my heart beat so quickly that sometimes I was actually concerned that I might have a heart attack or faint. My fear of being judged on account of my awkwardness and noticeable physiological-arousal symptoms eventually stopped me from leaving my room altogether. After a while, I completely stopped attending classes. Many days, I'd set my alarm, get up, get dressed, have some cereal, pack my books, and get ready for class, only to stand by my door inside my room shaking uncontrollably and unable to open the door to take the step into the hallway. Over the next three months between October and December, I lost thirty pounds, because eating alone at meal hall induced too many negative thoughts and too much shaking, sweating, and blushing when I thought others were watching me eat. The only times I'd leave my room to go to the bathroom or take showers was after 3 a.m., which allowed me to avoid other people. Knowing that I was hurting myself both academically and physically just increased my anxiety even further, because I didn't know how to help myself.

Despite knowing that my fears were irrational, I remained utterly crippled by my anxiety. Eventually, I became so depressed that I attempted suicide. My week spent in a psychiatric ward was my rock bottom. Prior to this point, I had never admitted to anyone that I needed help with my anxiety. I was too embarrassed and fearful of what others would think. Upon my hospital release, however, things began to change.

I didn't receive any treatment per se while I was in the hospital. I was there for a week with no extra clothes, deodorant, or toothpaste and saw a psychiatrist for a total of maybe twenty minutes. I was advised to meet with a local psychiatrist upon my release, which I did. Over the next two years I saw a social worker, three psychiatrists, and four psychologists. I didn't feel comfortable talking to anyone, and I rarely saw any of them more than a few times. First, I was prescribed the antidepressant Celexa, but I experienced some side effects, such as hyperarousal and tremors. I was only on this medication for a few months because the trembling was an obvious issue for me, considering how socially anxious I was. My extreme concern that people in my classes would notice my trembling seemed to make the medication's side effects even worse, so I decided to go off Celexa. Next, I was prescribed Prozac, which I took for almost two years with absolutely no results. I didn't experience any side effects with this medication (thank goodness!), but there were no positive benefits either. Finally, things started to turn around in my third year of university. I was prescribed Effexor, and noticed some positive effects in both my mood and my anxiety within the first three months. And after taking the medication for a few months, I received a phone call inviting me to participate in a study designed to test a brief cognitive-behavioral group intervention for reducing anxiety sensitivity in university students.

Although the program sounded really interesting and I agreed to participate, I almost didn't show up the first day. I managed to convince myself that this could be good for me, even though thinking about the group format filled me with dread. Interestingly, however, I often had more anxiety around familiar people than strangers. For instance, the idea of eating alone at meal hall and seeing people from my floor of the dorm terrified me for fear of what they'd think of my having no friends. The idea of a stranger seeing me alone was also uncomfortable but not nearly as much as someone who knew me, even if only slightly. As I saw it, someone who knew me and saw me sitting alone would now label me as a loser. In preparing myself to participate in the program, I reminded myself that I just might learn how to better manage my anxiety.

*On the first day, I met the two group facilitators and six other par-
ticipants. I appreciated that the group wasn't too big. After signing forms
indicating our informed consent to participate and our agreement to maintain others' confidentiality, we filled out a number of questionnaires. Then
we were introduced to the psychoeducation component of the program. We
learned about the anxiety cycle and received a lot of useful information on
how exposure to anxiety-related sensations (stressful situations) can trigger
negative cognitions (such as catastrophizing) about potentially hazardous
outcomes (such as a heart attack or being rejected) in people who are particularly sensitive to such sensations. I was quite certain that I was one of those
people. Indeed, I scored high on the Anxiety Sensitivity Index (Peterson and
Reiss 1992). In particular, I reported significant social and physical concerns
related to anxiety but fewer psychological concerns.*

*On the second day, we learned how certain types of thinking errors,
coupled with sensitivity to anxiety-related sensations, could increase our
risk of having more-intense anxiety and even panic attacks. The facilitators
showed us how to identify these thinking errors or "dysfunctional thoughts."
We learned that the two most common types of thinking errors for anxiety-
sensitive people are "probability overestimation" and "catastrophic thinking."
We were instructed in ways to challenge these dysfunctional thoughts by
examining the evidence ("What are the chances" that a harmful consequence,
such as fainting, will ensue?), de-catastrophizing ("What if" you did faint?),
and substituting anxiety-provoking cognitions with more-reasonable thoughts
("What else" could you think? What's another way of looking at it?).*

*Somewhat to our surprise, on the third day of the group, we were asked
to meet the facilitators in one of the campus gyms. At the gym, we engaged in
ten minutes of running, after which we were assessed for current physical sensations and our reactions to these sensations, such as feelings of breathlessness,
suffocation, losing control, numbness, and so forth. The facilitators explained
the rationale for doing the running as an "interoceptive" technique designed
to expose us to sensations that resemble anxiety, sensations that can be frightening for highly sensitive people. It seems that some people who are particularly sensitive to anxiety-related sensations tend to avoid activities that can
induce such sensations (such as sex and exercise). Apparently, it's thought that
reduced aerobic fitness might actually contribute to development of AS, panic
attacks, and even panic disorder. The more I thought about this, the more
it made sense to me. I began to wonder whether all my physical activity as
a child and adolescent had actually protected me from severe anxiety and*

whether I'd lost that protective effect when I'd quit soccer in high school. I realized that since coming to university, I hadn't participated in any physical activity at all. In fact, many days I hadn't even walked across campus!

At the end of the third session, we were given a homework assignment in which we were asked to complete ten minutes of running on at least ten additional occasions prior to coming back for a three-month follow-up session. After each running session, we were to complete the same assessment of physical sensations and our reactions to them. At first, I was quite bothered by the sensations, and on that first day in the gym, I even worried that others in the group would notice how breathless I was after the exercise and think I was really strange because of how I gasped for breath. But eventually, with practice at running, in many ways this became the most enjoyable part of the program. Doing the running exercise came to remind me of all the fun I used to have playing soccer. I began to think that maybe I could check out the university's intramural soccer program or just start a running routine.

Three months later, group members participated in a follow-up session. At this session, we completed the same questionnaires again. This allowed the researchers to test the effectiveness of the program in reducing AS levels by comparing where we were after the program relative to where we were before we started. At follow-up, we were asked to provide feedback about the program and suggestions for improvement. I told them how much I liked the simple questions: "What's the worst that can happen?" "What are the chances that the worst-case scenario will happen?" "What if it does happen—so what?" "What else can I think right now instead of thinking the worst?" I told them that I really liked the "So what?" question and that I used it a lot. I told them how I had started creating situations such as walking across the front of the class to put something in the garbage can to say to myself, "So what if they're looking at me?" "So what if they notice that I'm shaking?" Eventually, I found that I could drop the second question, because I wasn't really shaking anymore! Another situation that I created to practice these challenges involved pushing myself to respond to questions in class. That way, I could say to myself afterward, "So what if I sounded nervous?" I even started going to the gym occasionally, partly so I could say to myself, "What if I did look a bit awkward on the treadmill? So what?" I found the phrase to be liberating. I told the facilitators that I'd come to enjoy the running and planned on continuing to run.

Over the past year, I've continued to struggle with anxiety but made significant progress. I still hear the little voice in the back of my head telling me that I'm being judged, that people find me socially awkward, or that people notice my nervousness, but I drown out that voice with positive self-talk. I find that it really helps me to reaffirm the irrationality of the initial negative thoughts. Now, when I enter a stressful or anxiety-provoking social situation, I ask myself: What's the worst-case scenario? What are the odds that it's likely to occur? And what if it did? So what? Would I never be able to get over it? Of course, I would.

Between challenging my thoughts, practicing breathing exercises, and running for both physical and psychological health, I'm doing much better. With regard to my AS, I'm not so frightened by the physical sensations, maybe in part because I'm much more physically active. I still have a lot of social concerns related to anxiety, but now I have more tools for coping with them. Probably the biggest difference now is that I force myself to deal with my anxiety rather than avoid it. I face my fears. I also try to maintain my sense of humor. I tell myself that I'm just like Charlie Brown: "I've developed a new philosophy: I only dread one day at a time."

CHAPTER SUMMARY

We must face what we fear; that is the case of
the core of the restoration of health.

—Max Lerner

Colette's story illustrates some of the benefits of participating in the brief cognitive behavioral program for reducing AS described in this book. All cognitive and behavioral programs are designed to promote people's learning the skills necessary for dealing with their particular challenges, for example, anxiety, depression, or personality problems. Skills are tools like can openers, hammers, and table saws. As with other tools, some we may use every day (such as cognitive challenging and diaphragmatic breathing), while others we may employ more strategically (for example, we may only need to do interoceptive-exposure exercises several times a week). In any case, the more research-tested tools we have in our toolbox, the better able we'll be to deal with a range of anxiety-provoking situations. If we practice our skills regularly, these tools will stay in better condition and not get rusty.

As discussed in chapter 1, anxiety sensitivity is an established risk factor for anxiety and related disorders. Finding an effective way of reducing AS offers people the potential to reduce the risk of developing more-debilitating problems, such as panic attacks, depression, substance abuse, health anxiety, and pain-related anxiety. We hope that through reading this book, you, like Colette, have found some useful tools for filling your toolbox, tools that will help you tackle your anxiety sensitivity.

Resources

AUDIOVISUAL

Ross, J. 2001. *Freedom from Anxiety.* Chicago: Nightingale-Conant. Available at http://www.rosscenter.com. This is a comprehensive self-help version of a program offered at the Ross Center for Anxiety and Related Disorders in Washington, DC.

BOOKS

Barlow, D. H., and M. G. Craske. 2007. *Mastery of Your Anxiety and Panic.* 4th ed. New York: Oxford University Press.

Bourne, E. J. 2000. *The Anxiety and Phobia Workbook.* 3rd ed. Oakland, CA: New Harbinger Publications, Inc.

Burns, D. D. 1999. *The Feeling Good Handbook.* Revised ed. New York: Plume.

Greenberger, D., and C. A. Padesky. 1995. *Mind Over Mood: Change How You Feel by Changing the Way You Think.* New York: The Guilford Press.

Ross, J. 1995. *Triumph Over Fear: A Book of Help and Hope for People with Anxiety, Panic Attacks, and Phobias.* New York: Bantam.

Additional self-help books and tape programs are listed in the Anxiety Disorders Association of America's online bookstore at http://www.adaa.org.

NATIONAL ORGANIZATIONS

Anxiety Disorders Association of America (ADAA)
http://www.adaa.org

Anxiety Disorders Association of Canada (ADAC)
http://www.anxietycanada.ca

American Psychological Association (APA)
http://www.apa.org

Association for Behavioral and Cognitive Therapies (ABCT)
http://www.abct.org

The British Psychological Society
http://www.bps.org.uk

Canadian Psychological Association (CPA)
http://www.cpa.ca

National Institute of Mental Health
http://nimh.nih.gov

References

Addy, K. B. E. 2007. The treatment of depression and anxiety within the context of chronic obstructive pulmonary disease. *Clinical Case Studies* 6 (5):383–93.

Adler, C. M., M. G. Craske, and D. H. Barlow. 1987. Relaxation-induced panic (RIP): When resting isn't peaceful. *Integrative Psychiatry* 5 (2):94–100.

Agosti, V., E. Nunes, and F. Levin. 2002. Rates of psychiatric comorbidity among U.S. residents with lifetime cannabis dependence. *American Journal of Drug and Alcohol Abuse* 28 (4):643–52.

American Psychiatric Association. 1980. *Diagnostic and Statistical Manual of Mental Disorders (DSM-III)*. 3rd ed. Washington, DC: American Psychiatric Publishing, Inc.

———. 1994. *Diagnostic and Statistical Manual of Mental Disorders (DSM-IV)*. 4th ed. Washington, DC: American Psychiatric Publishing, Inc.

———. 2000. *Diagnostic and Statistical Manual of Mental Disorders (DSM-IV-TR)*. 4th ed. Washington, DC: American Psychiatric Publishing, Inc.

Anderson, D. E., and M. A. Chesney. 2002. Gender-specific association of perceived stress and inhibited breathing pattern. *International Journal of Behavioral Medicine* 9 (3):216–27.

Antony, M. M., D. R. Ledley, A. Liss, and R. P. Swinson. 2006. Responses to symptom induction exercises in panic disorder. *Behaviour Research and Therapy* 44 (1):85–98.

Asmundson, G. J. G., and G. R. Norton. 1995. Anxiety sensitivity in patients with physically unexplained chronic back pain: A preliminary report. *Behaviour Research and Therapy* 33 (7):771–77.

Asmundson, G. J. G., P. J. Norton, and F. Veloso. 1999. Anxiety sensitivity and fear of pain with recurring headaches. *Behaviour Research and Therapy* 37 (8):703–13.

Asmundson, G. J. G., and M. B. Stein. 1994. Selective processing of social threat in patients with generalized social phobia: Evaluation using a dot-probe paradigm. *Journal of Anxiety Disorders* 8 (2):107–17.

Asmundson, G. J. G., and S. Taylor. 1996. Role of anxiety sensitivity in pain-related fear and avoidance. *Journal of Behavioral Medicine* 19 (6):577–86.

Asmundson, G. J. G., J. W. S. Vlaeyen, and G. Crombez. 2004. *Understanding and Treating Fear of Pain.* Oxford, England, UK: Oxford University Press, Inc.

Asmundson, G. J. G., K. D. Wright, and H. D. Hadjistavropoulos. 2005. Hypervigilance and attentional fixedness in chronic musculoskeletal pain: Consistency of findings across modified stroop and dot-probe tasks. *The Journal of Pain* 6 (8):497–506.

Atlantis, E., C. Chow, A. Kirby, and M. F. Singh. 2004. An effective exercise-based intervention for improving mental health and quality of life measures: A randomized controlled trial. *Preventive Medicine* 39 (2):424–34.

Baillie, A. J., and R. M. Rapee. 2004. Predicting who benefits from psychoeducation and self help for panic attacks. *Behavior Research and Therapy* 42 (5):513–27.

Ball, S. G., M. W. Otto, M. H. Pollack, R. Uccello, and J. F. Rosenbaum. 1995. Differentiating social phobia and panic disorder: A test of core beliefs. *Cognitive Therapy and Research* 19 (4):473–81.

Bandura, A. 1977. Self-efficacy: Toward a unifying theory of behavioral change. *Psychological Review* 84 (2):191–215.

————. 1986. *Social Foundations of Thought and Action: A Social Cognitive Theory.* Englewood Cliffs, NJ: Prentice-Hall, Inc.

————. 1994. Regulative function of perceived self-efficacy. In *Personnel selection and classification*, ed. M. G. Rumsey, C. B. Walker, and J. H. Harris, 261–71. Hillsdale, NJ: Lawrence Erlbaum Associates, Inc.

Barloon, T. J., and R. Noyes, Jr. 1997. Charles Darwin and panic disorder. *Journal of the American Medical Association* 277 (2):138–41.

Barlow, D. H. 1988. *Anxiety and Its Disorders: The Nature and Treatment of Anxiety and Panic.* 1st ed. New York: The Guilford Press.

————. 1997. Anxiety disorders, comorbid substance abuse, and benzodiazepine discontinuation: Implications for treatment. In *NIDA research monograph 172: Treatment of drug-dependent individuals with comorbid mental disorders.* Rockville, MD: National Institute on Drug Abuse.

————. 2002. *Anxiety and Its Disorders: The Nature and Treatment of Anxiety and Panic.* 2nd ed. New York: The Guilford Press.

Barlow, D. H., T. A. Brown, and M. G. Craske. 1994. Definitions of panic attacks and panic disorder in the DSM-IV: Implications for research. *Journal of Abnormal Psychology* 103 (3):553–64.

Barlow, D. H., and M. G. Craske. 2007. *Mastery of Your Anxiety and Panic.* 4th ed. New York: Oxford University Press, Inc.

Barlow, D. H., J. M. Gorman, M. K. Shear, and S. W. Woods. 2000. Cognitive-behavioral therapy, imipramine, or their combination for panic disorder: A randomized controlled trial. *The Journal of the American Medical Association* 283 (19):2529–36.

Beck, A. T. 1976. *Cognitive Therapy and the Emotional Disorders.* New York: International Universities Press.

Beck, J. S. 1995. *Cognitive Therapy: Basics and Beyond.* New York: Guilford Press.

Becker, E. S., V. Türke, S. Neumer, U. Soeder, and J. Margraf. 2002. Prevalence and correlates of specific phobias and specific fears in young women. Working paper.

Beitman, B. D., N. C. Beck, W. E. Deuser, C. S. Carter, J. R. Davidson, and R. J. Maddock. 1994. Patient stage of change predicts outcome in a panic disorder medication trial. *Anxiety* 1 (2):64–69.

Benjamin, R. S., E. J. Costello, and M. Warren. 1990. Anxiety disorders in a pediatric sample. *Journal of Anxiety Disorders* 4 (4):293–316.

Berczi, I. 1994. *Advances in Psychoneuroimmunology.* New York: Plenum Press, 1–15 (accessed May 15, 2008, at http://home.cc.umanitoba.ca/~berczii/page2.htm).

Bernstein, A., M. J. Zvolensky, R. Kotov, W. A. Arrindell, S. Taylor, B. Sandin, B. J. Cox, S. H. Stewart, M. Bouvard, S. J. Cardenas, G. H. Eifert, and N. B. Schmidt. 2006. Taxonicity of anxiety sensitivity: A multi-national analysis. *Journal of Anxiety Disorders* 20 (1):1–22.

Bernstein, A., M. J. Zvolensky, P.J. Norton, N. B. Schmidt, S. Taylor, J. P. Forsyth, S. F.. Lewis, M. T. Feldner, E. W. Leen-Feldner, S. H. Stewart, and B. Cox. 2007. Taxometric and factor analytic models of anxiety sensitivity: Integrating approaches to latent structural research. *Psychological Assessment* 19 (1):74–87.

Boecker, H., T. Sprenger, M. E. Spilker, G. Henriksen, M. Koppenhoefer, K. J. Wagner, M. Valet, A. Berthele, and T. R. Tolle. 2008. The runner's high: Opioidergic mechanisms in the human brain. *Cerebral Cortex*, advance print (doi:10.1093/cercor/bhn013).

Bolton, J., B. J. Cox, I. Clara, and J. Sareen. 2006. Use of alcohol and drugs to selfmedicate anxiety disorders in a nationally representative sample. *Journal of Nervous and Mental Disease* 194 (11):818–25.

Bonin, M. F., G. R. Norton, G. J. G. Asmundson, S. Dicurzio, and S. Pidlubney. 2000. Drinking away the hurt: The nature and prevalence of PTSD in substance abuse patients attending a community-based treatment program. *Journal of Behavior Therapy and Experimental Psychiatry* 31 (1):55–66.

Bonn-Miller, M. O., M. J. Zvolensky, and A. Bernstein. 2007. Marijuana use motives: Concurrent relations to frequency of past 30-day use and anxiety sensitivity among young adult marijuana smokers. *Addictive Behaviors* 32 (1):49–62.

Bonn-Miller, M. O., M. J. Zvolensky, E. C. Marshall, and A. Bernstein. 2007. Incremental validity of anxiety sensitivity in relation to marijuana withdrawal symptoms. *Addictive Behaviors* 32 (9):1843–51.

Bouton, M. E., S. Mineka, and D. H. Barlow. 2001. A modern learning theory perspective on the etiology of panic disorder. *Psychological Review* 108 (1):4–32.

Bowlby, J. 1988. *A Secure Base: Parent-Child Attachment and Healthy Human Development.* New York: Basic Books.

Breslau, N. 2002. Epidemiologic studies of trauma, posttraumatic stress disorder, and other psychiatric disorders. *The Canadian Journal of Psychiatry* 47 (10):923–29.

Breslau, N., and D. F. Klein. 1999. Smoking and panic attacks: An epidemiologic investigation. *Archives of General Psychiatry* 56 (12):1141–47.

Breslau, N., S. P. Novak, and R. C. Kessler. 2004. Psychiatric disorders and stages of smoking. *Biological Psychiatry* 55 (1):69–76.

Breslau, N., T. Roth, L. Rosenthal, and P. Andreski. 1996. Sleep disturbance and psychiatric disorders: A longitudinal epidemiological study of young adults. *Biological Psychiatry* 39 (6):411–18.

Broderick, P. C. 2005. Mindfulness and coping with dysphoric mood: Contrasts with rumination and distraction. *Cognitive Therapy and Research* 29 (5):501–10.

Broman-Fulks, J. J., M. E. Berman, B. A. Rabian, and M. J. Webster. 2004. Effects of aerobic exercise on anxiety sensitivity. *Behaviour Research and Therapy* 42 (2):125–36.

Broman-Fulks, J. J., M. S. McCloskey, and M. E. Berman. 2007. Anxiety sensitivity and retaliatory aggressive behavior in research volunteers. *Aggressive Behavior* 33 (2):137–44.

Bronson, W. C. 1966. Central orientations: A study of behavior organization from childhood to adolescence. *Child Development* 37 (1):125–55.

Broocks, A., B. Bandelow, G. Pekrun, A. George, T. F. Meyer, U. Bartmann, U. Hillmer-Vogel, and E. Rüther. 1998. Comparison of aerobic exercise, clomipramine, and placebo in the treatment of panic disorder. *American Journal of Psychiatry* 155 (5):603–09.

Broocks, A., T. F. Meyer, B. Bandelow, A. George, U. Bartmann, E. Rüther, and U. Hillmer-Vogel. 1997. Exercise avoidance and impaired endurance capacity in patients with panic disorder. *Neuropsychobiology* 36 (4):182–87.

Brown, T. A., and T. F. Cash. 1989. The phenomenon of panic in non-clinical populations: Further evidence and methodological considerations. *Journal of Anxiety Disorders* 3 (3):139–48.

Brownell, K. D., G. A. Marlatt, E. Lichtenstein, and G. T. Wilson. 1986. Understanding and preventing relapse. *American Psychologist* 41 (7):765–82.

Bruce, T. J., D. A. Spiegel, S. F. Gregg, and A. Nuzzarello. 1995. Predictors of alprazolam discontinuation with and without cognitive behavior therapy in panic disorder. *American Journal of Psychiatry* 152 (8):1156–60.

Bruce, T. J., D. A. Spiegel, and M. T. Hegel. 1999. Cognitive behavioral therapy helps prevent relapse and recurrence of panic disorder following alprazolam discontinuation: A long-term follow-up of the Peoria and Dartmouth studies. *Journal of Consulting and Clinical Psychology* 67 (1):151–56.

Buckner, J. D., M. O. Bonn-Miller, M. J. Zvolensky, and N. B. Schmidt. 2007. Marijuana use motives and social anxiety among marijuana-using young adults. *Addictive Behaviors* 32 (10):2238–52.

Budney, A. J., J. R. Hughes, B. A. Moore, and R. Vandrey. 2004. Review of the validity and significance of cannabis withdrawal syndrome. *American Journal of Psychiatry* 161 (11):1967–77.

Burns, D. D. 1989. *The Feeling Good Handbook.* New York: William Morrow and Company, Inc.

Byrne, A. E., and D. G. Byrne. 1993. The effect of exercise on depression, anxiety, and other mood states: A review. *Journal of Psychosomatic Research* 3 (6):565–74.

Campbell, A. K., and S. B. Matthews. 2005. Darwin's illness revealed. *Postgraduate Medical Journal* 81 (954):248–51.

Canadian Psychological Association. 2006. *What Is Depression?* (Accessed July 6, 2008, at http://www.cpa.ca/publications/yourhealthpsychology worksfactsheets/depression/Default.asp).

Capote, T. 1958. *Breakfast at Tiffany's: A Short Novel and Three Stories.* New York: Random House.

Centre for Addiction and for Mental Health (CAMH). 2007. *Change, Recovery, and Relapse Prevention.* (Accessed May 15, 2008, at http://www.camh.net/).

Chambless, D. L., and E. J. Gracely. 1989. Fear of fear and the anxiety disorders. *Cognitive Therapy and Research* 13 (1):9–20.

Clark, D. M. 1986. A cognitive approach to panic. *Behaviour Research and Therapy* 24 (4):461–70.

Comeau, N., S. H. Stewart, and P. Loba. 2001. The relations of trait anxiety, anxiety sensitivity and sensation seeking to adolescents' motivations for alcohol, cigarette and marijuana use. *Addictive Behaviors* 26 (6):803–25.

Compton, W. M., B. F. Grant, J. D. Colliver, M. D. Glantz, and F. S. Stinson. 2004. Prevalence of marijuana use disorders in the United States: 1991–1992 and 2001–2002. *Journal of the American Medical Association* 291 (17):2114–21.

Conrod, P. J. 2000. Personality, sensitivity to alcohol reinforcement, and family history of alcoholism: Different sources of motivation for substance use in high-risk and substance abusing individuals. *Dissertation Abstracts International, Section B: The Sciences and Engineering* 60 (12-B):6356.

———. 2006. The role of anxiety sensitivity in subjective and physio-logical responses to social and physical stressors. *Cognitive Behaviour Therapy* 35 (4):216–25.

Conrod, P. J., and S. H. Stewart. 2005. A critical look at dual-focused cognitive-behavioral treatments for comorbid substance use and psychiatric disorders: Strengths, limitations, and future directions. *Journal of Cognitive Psychotherapy* 19 (3):261–84.

Conrod, P. J., S. H. Stewart, R. O. Pihl, S. Côté, V. Fontaine, and M. Dongier. 2000. Efficacy of brief coping skills interventions that match different personality profiles of female substance abusers. *Psychology of Addictive Behaviors* 14 (3):231–42.

Cox, B. J. 1999. The role of anxiety sensitivity in panic and other disorders (summary). Program abstracts of the 19th National Conference of the Anxiety Disorders Association of America (ADAA) 24:86.

Cox, B. J., S. C. Borger, and M. W. Enns. 1999. Anxiety sensitivity and emotional disorders: Psychometric studies and their theoretical implications. In *Anxiety sensitivity: Theory, research, and treatment of the fear of anxiety*, ed. S. Taylor, 115–48. Mahwah, NJ: Lawrence Erlbaum Associates, Inc.

Cox, B. J., N. S. Endler, and R. P. Swinson. 1991. Clinical and nonclinical panic attacks: An empirical test of a panic-anxiety continuum. *Journal of Anxiety Disorders* 5 (1):21–34.

Cox, B. J., M. W. Enns, and S. Taylor. 2001. The effect of rumination as a mediator of elevated anxiety sensitivity in major depression. *Cognitive Therapy and Research* 25 (5):525–34.

Craske, M. G. 1999. *Anxiety Disorders: Psychological Approaches to Theory and Treatment*. Boulder, CO: Westview Press.

Craske, M. G., M. Rowe, M. Lewin, and R. Noriega-Dimitri. 1997. Interoceptive exposure versus breathing retraining within cognitive-behavioural therapy for panic disorder with agoraphobia. *The British Journal of Clinical Psychology* 36 (1):85–99.

Crombez, G., J. W. Vlaeyen, P. H. Heuts, and R. Lysens. 1999. Pain-related fear is more disabling than pain itself: Evidence on the role of pain-related fear in chronic back pain disability. *Pain* 80 (1):329–39.

Deacon, B., J. Lickel, and J. S. Abramowitz. 2008. Medical utilization across the anxiety disorders. *Journal of Anxiety Disorders* 22 (2):344–50.

Dick, R. W., S. M. Manson, and J. Beals. 1993. Alcohol use among male and female Native American adolescents: Patterns and correlates of student drinking in a boarding school. *Journal of Studies on Alcohol* 54 (2):172–77.

DiClemente, C. C., J. O. Prochaska, S. K. Fairhurst, W. F. Velicer, M. M. Velasquez, and J. S. Rossi. 1991. The process of smoking cessation: An analysis of precontemplation, contemplation, and preparation stages of change. *Journal of Consulting and Clinical Psychology* 59 (2):295–304.

DiLorenzo, T. M., E. P. Bargman, R. Stucky-Ropp, G. S. Brassington, P. A. Frensch, and T. LaFontaine. 1999. Long-term effects of aerobic exercise on psychological outcomes. *Preventive Medicine* 28 (1):75–85.

Dixon, N. F. 1980. Humor: A cognitive alternative to stress? In *Stress and anxiety* vol. 7, ed. I. G. Sarason and C. D. Spielberger, 281–89. Washington, DC: Hemisphere.

Donnell, C. D., and R. J. McNally. 1990. Anxiety sensitivity and panic attacks in a nonclinical population. *Behaviour Research and Therapy* 28 (1):83–85.

Dozois, D. J. A., H. A. Westra, K. A. Collins, T. S. Fung, and J. K. F. Garry. 2004. Stages of change in anxiety: Psychometric properties of the University of Rhode Island Change Assessment (URICA) scale. *Behaviour Research and Therapy* 42 (6):711–29.

Dratcu, L. 2001. Physical exercise: An adjunctive treatment for panic disorder? *European Psychiatry* 16 (6):372–74.

Dunn, A. L., M. H. Trivedi, and H. A. O'Neal. 2001. Physical activity dose-response effects on outcomes of depression and anxiety. *Medicine and Science in Sports and Exercise* 33 (Suppl. 6):S587–S597.

Ehlers, A. 1995. A 1-year prospective study of panic attacks: Clinical course and factors associated with maintenance. *Journal of Abnormal Psychology* 104 (1):164–72.

Ermalinski, R., P. G. Hanson, B. Lubin, J. I. Thornby, and P. A. Nahormek. 1997. Impact of a body-mind treatment component on alcoholic inpatients. *Journal of Psychosocial Nursing and Mental Health* 35 (7):39–45.

Fauerbach, J. A., J. W. Lawrence, J. A. Haythornthwaite, and L. Richter. 2002. Coping with the stress of a painful medical procedure. *Behaviour Research and Therapy* 40 (9):1003–15.

Fedoroff, I. C., S. Taylor, G. J. G. Asmundson, and W. J. Koch. 2000. Cognitive factors in traumatic stress reactions: Predicting PTSD symptoms from anxiety sensitivity and beliefs about harmful events. *Behavioural and Cognitive Psychotherapy* 28 (1):5–15.

Forsyth, J. P., G. H. Eifert, and R. N. Thompson. 1996. Systemic alarms in fear conditioning II: An experimental methodology using 20% carbon dioxide inhalation as an unconditioned stimulus. *Behavior Therapy* 27 (3):391–415.

Freeman, A., J. Pretzer, B. Fleming, and K. M. Simon. 1990. *Clinical Applications of Cognitive Therapy*. 1st ed. New York: Plenum Press.

Graves, R. 1960. *Goodbye to All That*. Harmondsworth, England, UK: Penguin Books.

Hadjistavropoulos, H. D., G. J. G. Asmundson, and K. M. Kowalyk. 2004. Measures of anxiety: Is there a difference in their ability to predict functioning at three-month follow-up among pain patients? *European Journal of Pain* 8 (1):1–11.

Hagh-Shenas, H., M. A. Goodarzi, G. Dehbozorgi, and H. Farashbandi. 2005. Psychological consequences of the Bam earthquake on professional and nonprofessional helpers. *Journal of Traumatic Stress* 18 (5):477–83.

Harber, V. J., and J. R. Sutton. 1984. Endorphins and exercise. *Sports Medicine* 1 (2):154–71.

Harte, J. L., and G. H. Eifert. 1995. The effects of running, environment, and attentional focus on athletes' catecholamine and cortisol levels and mood. *Psychophysiology* 32 (1):49–54.

Harvey, A. G., and S. Payne. 2002. The management of unwanted pre-sleep thoughts in insomnia: Distraction with imagery versus general distraction. *Behaviour Research and Therapy* 40 (3):267–77.

Hazen, A. L., J. R. Walker, and M. B. Stein. 1995. Comparison of anxiety sensitivity in panic disorder and social phobia. *Anxiety* 1 (6):298–301.

Health Canada. 2007. *Canada's Food Guide*. Ottawa, Ontario, Canada: Publications (accessed May 15, 2008, at http://www.hc-sc.gc.ca/fn-an/food-guide-aliment/order-commander/index-eng.php).

————. 2007. *Physical Activity Guide*. Ottawa, Ontario, Canada: Publications.

Henman, L. D. 2001. Humor as a coping mechanism: Lessons from POWs. *Humor: International Journal of Humor Research* 14 (1):83–94.

Hinton, D. E., K. Um, and P. Ba. 2001. Kyol goeu ("wind overload") part I: A cultural syndrome of orthostatic panic among Khmer refugees. *Transcultural Psychiatry* 38 (4):403–32.

Hinton, D. E., V. Pich, S. A. Safren, M. H. Pollack, and R. J. McNally. 2006. Anxiety sensitivity among Cambodian refugees with panic disorder: A factor analytic investigation. *Journal of Anxiety Disorders* 20 (3):281–95.

Holloway, W., and R. J. McNally. 1987. Effects of anxiety sensitivity on the response to hyperventilation. *Journal of Abnormal Psychology* 96 (4):330–34.

Holmes, T. H., and R. H. Rahe. 1967. Holmes-Rahe life changes scale. *Journal of Psychosomatic Research* 11 (2):213–18.

Ingledew, D. K., D. Markland, and A. R. Medley. 1998. Exercise motives and stages of change. *Journal of Health Psychology* 3 (4):477–89.

Jakupcak, M., T. Osborne, S. Michael, J. Cook, P. Albrizio, and M. McFall. 2006. Anxiety sensitivity and depression: Mechanisms for understanding somatic complaints in veterans with posttraumatic stress disorder. *Journal of Traumatic Stress* 19 (4):471–79.

Kaiya, H., T. Umekage, S. Harada, Y. Okazaki, and T. Sasaki. 2005. Factors associated with the development of panic attack and panic disorder: Survey in the Japanese population. *Psychiatry and Clinical Neuroscience* 59 (2):177–82.

Kanner, A. D., J. C. Coyne, C. Schaefer, and R. S. Lazarus. 1981. Comparison of two models of stress measurement: Daily hassles and uplifts versus major life events. *Journal of Behavioral Medicine* 4 (1):1–39.

Keefe, F. J., M. E. Rumble, C. D. Scipio, L. A. Giordano, and L. M. Perri. 2004. Psychological aspects of persistent pain: Current state of the science. *The Journal of Pain* 5 (4):195–211.

Keogh, E., S. Ayers, and H. Francis. 2002. Does anxiety sensitivity predict post-traumatic stress symptoms following childbirth? A preliminary report. *Cognitive Behaviour Therapy* 31 (4):145–55.

Keogh, E., and J. Birkby. 1999. The effect of anxiety sensitivity and gender on the experience of pain. *Cognition and Emotion* 13 (6):813–29.

Keogh, E., and L. Mansoor. 2001. Investigating the effects of anxiety sensitivity and coping on the perception of cold pressor pain in healthy women. *European Journal of Pain* 5 (1):11–22.

Kerns, R. D., and R. Rosenberg. 2000. Predicting responses to self-management treatments for chronic pain: Application of the pain stages of change model. *Pain* 84 (1):49–55.

Kessler, R. C., P. Berglund, O. Demler, R. Jin, K. R. Merikangas, and E. E. Walters. 2005. Lifetime prevalence and age-of-onset distributions of DSM-IV disorders in the national comorbidity survey replication. *Archives of General Psychiatry* 62 (6):593–602.

Kessler, R. C., K. A. McGonagle, S. Zhao, C. B. Nelson, M. Hughes, S. Eshleman, H. U. Wittchen, and K. S. Kendler. 1994. Lifetime and 12-month prevalence of DSM-III-R psychiatric disorders in the United States: Results from the national comorbidity study. *Archives of General Psychiatry* 51 (1):8–19.

Kessler, R. C., A. Sonnega, E. Bromet, M. Hughes, and C. B. Nelson. 1995. Posttraumatic stress disorder in the National Comorbidity Survey. *Archives of General Psychiatry* 52 (12):1048–60.

Kilpatrick, D. G., C. L. Best, L. J. Veronen, A. E. Amick, L. A. Villeponteaux, and G. A. Ruff. 1985. Mental health correlates of criminal victimization: A random community survey. *Journal of Consulting and Clinical Psychology* 53 (6):866–73.

Kuch, K., B. J. Cox, R. Evans, and I. Shulman. 1994. Phobias, panic, and pain in 55 survivors of road vehicle accidents. *Journal of Anxiety Disorders* 8 (2):181–87.

Kuch, K., B. J. Cox, C. B. Woszczyna, R. P. Swinson, and I. Shulman. 1991. Chronic pain in panic disorder. *Journal of Behaviour Therapy and Experimental Psychiatry* 22 (4):255–59.

Kulka, R. A., W. E. Schlenger, J. A. Fairbank, R. L. Hough, B. K. Jordan, C. R. Marmar, D. S. Weiss, and D. A. Grady. 1990. *Trauma and the Vietnam War generation: Report of findings from the National Vietnam Veterans Readjustment Study.* Philadelphia, PA: Brunner/Mazel.

Kushner, M. G., K. Abrams, P. Thuras, K. L. Hanson, M. Brekke, and S. Sletten. 2005. Follow-up study of anxiety disorder and alcohol dependence in comorbid alcoholism treatment patients. *Alcoholism: Clinical and Experimental Research* 29 (8):1432–43.

Kushner, M. G., R. Krueger, B. Frye, and J. Peterson. 2008. Epidemiological perspectives on co-occurring anxiety disorder and substance use disorder. In *Anxiety and substance use disorders: The vicious cycle of comorbidity,* ed. S. H. Stewart and P. J. Conrod. New York: Springer Science and Business Media, LLC.

Kushner, M. G., P. Thuras, K. Abrams, M. Brekke, and L. Stritar. 2001. Anxiety mediates the association between anxiety sensitivity and coping-related drinking motives in alcoholism treatment patients. *Addictive Behaviors* 26 (6):869–85.

LaCoursiere, R. B., K. E. Godfrey, and L. M. Ruby. 1980. Traumatic neurosis in the etiology of alcoholism: Vietnam combat and other trauma. *American Journal of Psychiatry* 137 (8):966–68.

Lang, A. J., J. T. Sorrell, C. S. Rodgers, and M. M. Lebeck. 2006. Anxiety sensitivity as a predictor of labor pain. *European Journal of Pain* 10 (3):263–70.

Ley, R. 1992. The many faces of Pan: Psychological and physiological differences among three types of panic attacks. *Behaviour Research and Therapy* 30 (4):347–57.

Lickel, J., E. Nelson, A. Hayes, and B. Deacon. Forthcoming. Interoceptive exposure exercises for evoking depersonalization and derealization: A pilot study. *Journal of Cognitive Psychotherapy.*

Lilienfeld, S. O., and S. Penna. 2001. Anxiety sensitivity: Relations to psychopathy, DSM-IV personality disorder features, and personality traits. *Journal of Anxiety Disorders* 15 (5):367–93.

Lugenbehl, D. 2000. The golden mean. In *Concepts in ethics*, ed. D. Lugenbehl. N.p. (accessed May 15, 2008, at https://teach.lanecc.edu/lugenbehld/rel_202_religions_of_china_and_japan/files/Golden_Mean.htm).

MacDonald, A. B., J. M. Baker, S. H. Stewart, and M. Skinner. 2000. Effects of alcohol on the response to hyperventilation of participants high and low in anxiety sensitivity. *Alcoholism: Clinical and Experimental Research* 24 (11):1656–65.

Maller, R. G., and S. Reiss. 1992. Anxiety sensitivity in 1984 and panic attacks in 1987. *Journal of Anxiety Disorders* 6 (3):241–47.

Marcus, B. H., C. A. Eaton, J. S. Rossi, and L. L. Harlow. 1994. Self-efficacy, decision making, and stages of change: An integrative model of physical exercise. *Journal of Applied Social Psychology* 24 (6):489–508.

Marlatt, G. A. 1985. Abstinence and controlled drinking: Alternative treatment goals for alcoholism and problem drinking? *Bulletin of the Society of Psychologists in Addictive Behaviors* 4 (3):123–50.

Marlatt, G. A., and D. M. Donovan, ed. 2005. *Relapse Prevention: Maintenance Strategies in the Treatment of Addictive Behaviors.* 2nd ed. New York: The Guilford Press.

Marlatt, G. A., and J. R. Gordon. 1985. *Relapse Prevention.* New York: The Guilford Press.

Mazur, James E. 2002. *Learning and Behavior.* 5th ed. Upper Saddle River, NJ: Prentice Hall/Pearson Education.

McGonigal, K. 2005. The politics of breathing: Still liberating women, after all these years? e-Sutra: The Worldwide Yoga List, July 6 (accessed May 31, 2008, at http://esutra.blogspot.com/2005/07/politics-of-breathing-still-liberating.html).

McNaughton, N. 2008. The neurobiology of anxiety: Potential for co-morbidity of anxiety and substance use disorders. In *Anxiety and substance use disorders: The vicious cycle of comorbidity*, ed. S. H. Stewart and P. J. Conrod. New York: Springer Science and Business Media, LLC.

McWilliams, L. A., and G. J. G. Asmundson. 2001. Is there a negative association between anxiety sensitivity and arousal-increasing substances and activities? *Journal of Anxiety Disorders* 15 (3):161–70.

Mickelson, K. D., R. C. Kessler, and P. R. Shaver. 1997. Adult attachment in a nationally representative sample. *Journal of Personality and Social Psychology* 73 (5):1092–1106.

Montaigne, M. de. 1580. *The complete essays of Montaigne.* Translated by D. M. Frame. Stanford, CA: Stanford University Press, 1958.

Mullane, J. C., S. H. Stewart, E. Rhyno, D. Steeves, M. Watt, and A. Eisner. 2008. Anxiety sensitivity and difficulties with smoking cessation. In *Advances in Psychology Research*, vol. 54A, edited by A. M. Columbus. Hauppauge, NY: Nova Science Publishers.

Mystkowski, J. L., S. Mineka, L. L. Vernon, and R. E. Zinbarg. 2003. Changes in caffeine states enhance return of fear in spider phobia. *Journal of Consulting and Clinical Psychology* 71 (2):243–50.

National Sleep Foundation. 2005. Summary of findings (accessed May 15, 2008 at http://www.sleepfoundation.org).

Norton, G. R., B. J. Cox, P. L. Hewitt, and L. McLeod. 1997. Personality factors associated with generalized and non-generalized social anxiety. *Personality and Individual Differences* 22 (5):655–60.

Norton, G. R., B. J. Cox, and J. Malan. 1992. Nonclinical panickers: A critical review. *Clinical Psychology Review* 12 (2):121–39.

O'Connor, P. J., J. C. Smith, and W. P. Morgan. 2000. Physical activity does not provoke panic attacks in patients with panic disorder: A review of the evidence. *Anxiety, Stress, and Coping* 13 (4):333–53.

Ohayon, M. M. 1996. Epidemiological study on insomnia in the general population. *Sleep* 19 (3):S7–S15.

———. 1997. Prevalence of DSM-IV diagnostic criteria of insomnia: Distinguishing insomnia related to mental disorders from sleep disorders. *Journal of Psychiatric Research* 31 (3):333–46.

———. 2002. Epidemiology of insomnia: What we know and what we still need to learn. *Sleep Medicine Reviews* 6 (2):97–111.

Olson, G. A., R. D. Olson, and A. J. Kastin. 1996. Endogenous opiates: 1995. *Peptides* 17 (8):1421–66.

Otto, M. W. 2007. Interoceptive exposure in the treatment of panic and co-morbid disorders: Novel applications and mechanisms of action. Discussant for symposium presented at the 28th annual conference of the Anxiety Disorders Association of America (ADAA), March, Savannah, GA.

Otto, M. W., C. M. Demopulos, N. E. McLean, M. H. Pollack, and M. Fava. 1998. Additional findings on the association between anxiety sensitivity and hypochondriacal concerns: Examination of patients with major depression. *Journal of Anxiety Disorders* 12 (3):225–32.

Otto, M. W., M. H. Pollack, M. Fava, R. Uccello, and J. F. Rosenbaum. 1995. Elevated anxiety sensitivity index scores in patients with major depression: Correlates and changes with antidepressant treatment. *Journal of Anxiety Disorders* 9 (2):117–23.

Otto, M. W., M. H. Pollack, G. S. Sachs, and J. F. Rosenbaum. 1992. Hypochondriacal concerns, anxiety sensitivity, and panic disorder. *Journal of Anxiety Disorders* 6 (2):93–104.

Otto, M. W., M. B. Powers, and D. Fischmann. 2005. Emotional exposure in the treatment of substance use disorders: Conceptual model, evidence, and future directions. *Clinical Psychology Review* 25 (6):824–39.

Overholser, J. C., and E. H. Nasser. 2000. Cognitive-behavioral treatment for generalized anxiety disorder. *Journal of Contemporary Psychotherapy* 30 (2):149–61.

Palmer, J., N. Vacc, and J. Epstein. 1988. Adult inpatient alcoholics: Physical exercise as a treatment intervention. *Journal of Studies on Alcohol* 49 (5):418–21.

Parrish, I. S. 2003. *Military Veterans PTSD Reference Manual.* Bryn Mawr, PA: Infinity Publishing (retrieved on August 15, 2007, from http://www.ptsdmanual.com/).

Patton, G. C., C. Coffey, J. B. Carlin, L. Degenhardt, M. Lynskey, and W. Hall. 2002. Cannabis use and mental health in young people: Cohort study. *British Medical Journal* 325 (7374):1195–98.

Pavlov, I. P. 1927. *Conditioned Reflexes: An Investigation of the Physiological Activity of the Cerebral Cortex.* Oxford, England, UK: Oxford University Press.

Pecknold, J. C., R. P. Swinson, K. Kuch, and C. P. Lewis. 1988. Alprazolam in panic disorder and agoraphobia: Results from a multi-center trial: III. discontinuation effects. *Archives of General Psychiatry* 45 (5):429–36.

Peluso, M. A. M., and L. H. S. Guerra de Andrade. 2005. Physical activity and mental health: The association between exercise and mood. *Clinics* 60 (1):61–70.

Penedo, F. J., and J. R. Dahn. 2005. Exercise and well-being: A review of mental and physical health benefits associated with physical activity. *Current Opinion in Psychiatry* 18 (2):189–93.

Peterson, R. A., and S. Reiss. 1992. *Anxiety Sensitivity Index Revised Test Manual.* Worthington, OH: IDS Publishing Corporation.

Pina, A. A., and W. K. Silverman. 2004. Clinical phenomenology, somatic symptoms, and distress in Hispanic/Latino and European American youths with anxiety disorders. *Journal of Clinical Child and Adolescent Psychology* 33 (2):227–36.

Plotnikoff, R. C., C. Blanchard, S. B. Hotz, and R. Rhodes. 2001. Validation of the decisional balance scales in the exercise domain from the transtheoretical model: A longitudinal test. *Measurement in Physical Education and Exercise Science* 5 (4):191–206.

Prigerson, H. G., P. K. Maciejewski, and R. A. Rosenheck. 2002. Population attributable fractions of psychiatric disorders and behavioral outcomes associated with combat exposure among US men. *American Journal of Public Health* 92 (1):59–63.

Prochaska, J. O., and C. C. DiClemente. 1983. Stages and processes of self-change of smoking: Toward an integrative model of change. *Journal of Consulting and Clinical Psychology* 51 (3):390–95.

Prochaska, J. O., C. C. DiClemente, and J. C. Norcross. 1992. In search of how people change: Applications to addictive behaviors. *American Psychologist* 47 (9):1102–14.

Prochaska, J. O., and W. F. Velicer. 1997. The transtheoretical model of health behavior change. *American Journal of Health Promotion* 12 (1):38–48.

Proust, M. 1925. *The Guermantes Way*. New York: Modern Library.

Rachman, S. J. 1989. The return of fear: Review and prospect. *Clinical Psychology Review* 9 (2):147–68.

Ramsawh, H. J. 2006. Isolated sleep paralysis and its associations with anxiety sensitivity, history of trauma, paranormal beliefs, and life stress in a black sample. *Dissertation Abstracts International, Section B: The Sciences and Engineering* 66 (8-B):4497.

Rapee, R. M. 1994. Detection of somatic sensations in panic disorder. *Behaviour Research and Therapy* 32 (8):825–31.

Rapee, R. M., E. M. Litwin, and D. H. Barlow. 1990. Impact of life events on subjects with panic disorder and on comparison subjects. *American Journal of Psychiatry* 147 (5):640–44.

Rector, N. A., K. Szacun-Shimizu, and M. Leybman. 2007. Anxiety sensitivity within the anxiety disorders: Disorder-specific sensitivities and depression comorbidity. *Behaviour Research and Therapy* 45 (8):1967–75.

Redding, R. E., J. D. Herbert, E. M. Forman, and B. A. Gaudiano. Forthcoming. Popular self-help books for anxiety, depression, and trauma: How scientifically grounded and useful are they? *Professional Psychology: Research and Practice*.

Regier, D. A., W. E. Narrow, and D. S. Rae. 1990. The epidemiology of anxiety disorders: The Epidemiologic Catchment Area (ECA) experience. *Journal of Psychiatric Research* 24 (Suppl. 2):3–14.

Reid, J. C., S. S. Nair, S. I. Mistry, and B. D. Beitman. 1996. Effectiveness of stages of change and adinazolam SR in panic disorder: A neural network analysis. *Journal of Anxiety Disorders* 10 (5):331–45.

Reiss, S. 1991. Expectancy model of fear, anxiety, and panic. *Clinical Psychology Review* 11:141–53.

Reiss, S., and R. J. McNally. 1985. The expectancy model of fear. In *Theoretical issues in behavior therapy*, ed. S. Reiss and R. R. Bootzin, 107–21. New York: Academic Press.

Reiss, S., R. A. Peterson, D. M. Gursky, and R. J. McNally. 1986. Anxiety sensitivity, anxiety frequency, and the prediction of fearfulness. *Behaviour Research and Therapy* 24 (1):1–8.

Resnick, H. S., D. G. Kilpatrick, B. S. Dansky, B. E. Saunders, and C. L. Best. 1993. Prevalence of civilian trauma and posttraumatic stress disorder in a representative national sample of women. *Journal of Consulting and Clinical Psychology* 61 (6):984–91.

Robinson, S. A. 2005. A conceptual model of psychological distress in Native Americans. *Dissertation Abstracts International, Section B: The Sciences and Engineering* 65 (11-B):5629.

Rosenman, S., ed. 1938. *The Year of Crisis, 1933.* Vol. 2 of *The public papers of Franklin D. Roosevelt.* New York: Random House.

Roth, T., S. Jaeger, R. Jin, A. Kalsekar, P. E. Stang, and R. C. Kessler. 2006. Sleep problems, comorbid mental disorders, and role functioning in the national comorbidity survey replication. *Biological Psychiatry* 60 (12):1364–71.

Roy-Byrne, P. P., M. Geraci, and T. W. Uhde. 1986. Life events and the onset of panic disorder. *American Journal of Psychiatry* 143 (11):1424–27.

Rutter, M. 1997. Clinical implications of attachment concepts: Retrospect and prospect. In *Attachment and psychopathology*, ed. L. Atkinson and K. J. Zucker, 17–46. New York: The Guilford Press.

Sabourin, B. C., S. H. Stewart, S. B. Sherry, M. C. Watt, J. Wald, and V. V. Grant. Forthcoming. Physical exercise as interoceptive exposure within a brief cognitive behavioral treatment for anxiety sensitive women. *Journal of Cognitive Psychotherapy.*

Sallis, J. F., M. F. Hovell, C. R. Hofstetter, J. P. Elder, P. Faucher, V. M. Spry, E. Barrington, and M. Hackley. 1990. Lifetime history of relapse from exercise. *Addictive Behaviors* 15 (6):573–79.

Salmon, P. 2001. Effects of physical exercise on anxiety, depression, and sensitivity to stress: A unifying theory. *Clinical Psychology Review* 21 (1):33–61.

Sanderson, W. C., R. M. Rapee, and D. H. Barlow. 1989. The influence of an illusion of control on panic attacks induced via inhalation of

5.5% carbon dioxide-enriched air. *Archives of General Psychiatry* 46 (2):157–62.

Scher, C. D., and M. B. Stein. 2003. Developmental antecedents of anxiety sensitivity. *Journal of Anxiety Disorders* 17 (3):253–69.

Schmidt, N. B., J. D. Buckner, and M. E. Keough. 2007. Anxiety sensitivity as a prospective predictor of alcohol use disorders. *Behavior Modification* 31 (2):202–19.

Schmidt, N. B., R. Kotov, D. R. Lerew, T. E. Joiner, and N. S. Ialongo. 2005. Evaluating latent discontinuity in cognitive vulnerability to panic: A taxometric investigation. *Cognitive Therapy and Research* 29 (6):673–90.

Schmidt, N. B., D. R. Lerew, and R. J. Jackson. 1997. The role of anxiety sensitivity in the pathogenesis of panic: Prospective evaluation of spontaneous panic attacks during acute stress. *Journal of Abnormal Psychology* 106 (3):355–64.

Schmidt, N. B., D. R. Lerew, and R. J. Jackson. 1999. Prospective evaluation of anxiety sensitivity in the pathogenesis of panic: Replication and extension. *Journal of Abnormal Psychology* 108 (3):532–37.

Schmidt, N. B., and J. Trakowski. 2004. Interoceptive assessment and exposure in panic disorder: A descriptive study. *Cognitive and Behavioral Practice* 11:81–92.

Segal, Z. V., J. M. G. Williams, and J. D. Teasdale. 2002. *Mindfulness-Based Cognitive Therapy for Depression: A New Approach to Preventing Relapse*. New York: The Guilford Press.

Selye, H. 1946. The general adaptation syndrome and the diseases of adaptation. *Journal of Clinical Endocrinology* 6:117–230.

———. 1955. Stress and disease. *Science* 122:625–31.

Shepherd, R. J., M. H. Cox, and K. Simper. 1981. An analysis of "PAR-Q" responses in an office population. *Canadian Journal of Public Health* 72 (1):37–40.

Shostak, B. B., and R. A. Peterson. 1990. Effects of anxiety sensitivity on emotional response to a stress task. *Behaviour Research and Therapy* 28:513–21.

Siegel, J. M. 2003. Why we sleep. *Scientific American* 289 (5):92–97.

Sigmon, S. T., D. M. Dorhofer, K. J. Rohan, and N. E. Boulard. 2000. The impact of anxiety sensitivity, bodily expectations, and cultural beliefs on menstrual symptom reporting: A test of the menstrual reactivity hypothesis. *Journal of Anxiety Disorders* 14 (6):615–33.

Sigmon, S. T., C. Fink, K. J. Rohan, and L. T. Hotovy. 1996. Anxiety sensitivity and menstrual cycle reactivity: Psychophysiological and self-report differences. *Journal of Anxiety Disorders* 10 (5):393–410.

Silverman, W. K., and C. F. Weems. 1999. Anxiety sensitivity in children. In *Anxiety sensitivity: Theory, research and treatment of the fear of anxiety*, ed. S. Taylor, 239–68. Mahwah, NJ: Lawrence Erlbaum Associates, Inc.

Sinyor, D., S. G. Schwartz, F. Peronnet, G. Brisson, and P. Seraganian. 1983. Aerobic fitness level and reactivity to psychosocial stress: Physiological, biochemical, and subjective measures. *Psychosomatic Medicine* 45 (3):205–17.

Skinner, B. F. 1938. *The Behaviour of Organisms: An Experimental Analysis.* Oxford, England, UK: Appleton-Century.

Smits, J. A. J., M. B. Powers, A. C. Berry, and M. W. Otto. 2007. Translating empirically supported strategies into accessible interventions: The potential utility of exercise for the treatment of panic disorder. *Cognitive and Behavioural Practice* 14 (4):364–74.

Smits, J. A. J., and M. J. Zvolensky. 2006. Emotional vulnerability as a function of physical activity among individuals with panic disorder. *Depression and Anxiety* 23 (2):102–06.

Snyder, C. R., S. S. Ilardi, J. Cheavens, S. T. Michael, L. Yamhure, and S. Sympson. 2000. The role of hope in cognitive-behavior therapies. *Cognitive Therapy and Research* 24 (6):747–62.

Snyder, C. R., L. M. Irving, and J. R. Anderson. 1991. Hope and health. In *Handbook of social and clinical psychology: The health perspective*, ed. C. R. Snyder and D. R. Forsyth, 285–305. Elmsford, NY: Pergamon Press.

Stathopoulou, G., M. B. Powers, A. C. Berry, J. A. J. Smits, and M. W. Otto. 2006. Exercise interventions for mental health: A quantitative and qualitative review. *Clinical Psychology: Science and Practice* 13 (2):179–93.

Stein, M. B., K. L. Jang, and W. J. Livesley. 1999. Heritability of anxiety sensitivity: A twin study. *American Journal of Psychiatry* 156:246–51.

Stein, M. B., L. J. Torgrud, and J. R. Walker. 2000. Social phobia symptoms, subtypes, and severity: Findings from a community survey. *Archives of General Psychiatry* 57 (11):1046–52.

Stetson, B. A., A. O. Beacham, S. J. Frommelt, K. N. Boutelle, J. D. Cole, C. H. Ziegler, and S. W. Looney. 2005. Exercise slips in high-risk situations and activity patterns in long-term exercisers: An application of the relapse prevention model. *Annals of Behavioral Medicine* 30 (1):25–35.

Stewart, P. K., Y. P. Wu, and M. C. Roberts. 2007. Top producers of scholarly publications in clinical psychology PhD programs. *Journal of Clinical Psychology* 63 (12):1209–15.

Stewart, S. H. 1996. Alcohol abuse in individuals exposed to trauma: A critical review. *Psychological Bulletin* 120:83–112.

———. 1997. Trauma memory and alcohol abuse: Drinking to forget? In *Recollections of trauma: Scientific evidence and clinical practice*, ed. J. D. Read and D. S. Lindsay, 461–67. New York: Plenum Press.

Stewart, S. H., and G. J. G. Asmundson. 2006. Anxiety sensitivity and its impact on pain experiences and conditions: A state of the art. *Cognitive Behaviour Therapy* 35 (4):185–88.

Stewart, S. H., S. E. Buffett-Jerrott, and R. Kokoram. 2001. Heartbeat awareness and heart rate reactivity in anxiety sensitivity: A further investigation. *Journal of Anxiety Disorders* 15 (6):535–53.

Stewart, S. H., and P. J. Conrod. 2003. Psychosocial models of functional associations between posttraumatic stress disorder and substance use disorder. In *Trauma and substance abuse: Causes, consequences, and treatment of comorbid disorders*, ed. P. Ouimette and P. J. Brown, 29–55. Washington, DC: American Psychological Association.

———, ed. 2008. *Anxiety and Substance Use Disorders: The Vicious Cycle of Comorbidity*. New York: Springer Science and Business Media, LLC.

Stewart, S. H., P. J. Conrod, M. L. Gignac, and R. O. Pihl. 1998. Selective processing biases in anxiety-sensitive men and women. *Cognition and Emotion* 12 (1):105–33.

Stewart, S. H., K. Knize, and R. O. Pihl. 1992. Anxiety sensitivity and dependency in clinical and non-clinical panickers and controls. *Journal of Anxiety Disorders* 6 (2):119–31.

Stewart, S. H., and M. G. Kushner. 2001. Introduction to the special issues on "anxiety sensitivity and addictive behaviors." *Addictive Behaviors* 26 (6):775–85.

Stewart, S. H., and R. O. Pihl. 1994. Effects of alcohol administration on psychophysiological and subjective-emotional responses to aversive stimulation in anxiety-sensitive women. *Psychology of Addictive Behaviors* 8 (1):29–42.

Stewart, S. H., S. B. Samoluk, and A. B. MacDonald. 1999. Anxiety sensitivity and substance use and abuse. In *Anxiety sensitivity: Theory, research, and treatment of the fear of anxiety*, ed. S. Taylor, 287–319. Mahwah, NJ: Lawrence Erlbaum Associates, Inc.

Stewart, S. H., S. Taylor, and J. M. Baker. 1997. Gender differences in dimensions of anxiety sensitivity. *Journal of Anxiety Disorders* 11 (2):179–200.

Stewart, S. H., S. Taylor, K. L. Jang, B. J. Cox, M. C. Watt, I. C. Fedoroff, and S. C. Borger. 2001. Casual modeling of relations among learning history, anxiety sensitivity, and panic attacks. *Behaviour Research and Therapy* 39 (4):443–56.

Stewart, S. H., and M. C. Watt. 2000. Illness attitudes scale dimensions and their associations with anxiety-related constructs in a nonclinical sample. *Behaviour Research and Therapy* 38 (1):83–99.

———. 2001. Assessment of health anxiety. In *Health anxiety: Clinical research perspectives on hypochondriasis and related disorders*, ed. G. J. G. Asmundson, S. Taylor, and B. J. Cox. West Sussex, England, UK: John Wiley & Sons, Ltd.

Stewart, S. H., M. J. Zvolensky, and G. H. Eifert. 2001. Negative-reinforcement drinking motives mediate the relation between anxiety sensitivity and increased drinking behavior. *Personality and Individual Differences* 31 (2):157–71.

Stossel, S. 1998. Aches and pains: Like many great thinkers, William James was troubled in body and mind. *The Boston Phoenix*, March 26–April 2 ((accessed May 15, 2008, http://weeklywire.com/ww /03-30-98/boston_books_2.html).

Sullivan, M. J., B. Thorn, J. A. Haythornthwaite, F. Keefe, M. Martin, L. A. Bradley, and J. C. Lefebvre. 2001. Theoretical perspectives on the relation between catastrophizing and pain. *Clinical Journal of Pain* 17 (1):52–64.

Szabo, A. 2007. Comparison of the psychological effects of exercise and humor. In *Mood and human performance: Conceptual, measurement and applied issues*, ed. A. M. Lane, 201–16. Hauppauge, NY: Nova Science Publishers.

Taylor, S. 1999. *Anxiety Sensitivity: Theory, Research, and Treatment of the Fear of Anxiety*. Mahwah, NJ: Lawrence Erlbaum Associates, Inc.

———. 2004. *Advances in the Treatment of Posttraumatic Stress Disorder: Cognitive Behavioral Perspectives*. New York: Springer Publishing Co., Inc.

Taylor, S., K. L. Jang, S. H. Stewart, and M. B. Stein. 2008. Etiology of the dimensions of anxiety sensitivity: A behavioral-genetic analysis. *Journal of Anxiety Disorders* 22:899–914.

Taylor, S. E., L. C. Klein, B. P. Lewis, T. L. Gruenewald, R. A. Gurung, and J. A. Updegraff. 2000. Biobehavioral responses to stress in females: tend-and-befriend, not fight-or-flight. *Psychological Review* 107 (3):411–29.

Taylor, S. and W. J. Koch. 1995. Anxiety disorders due to motor vehicle accidents: Nature and treatment. *Clinical Psychology Review* 15 (8):721–38.

Taylor, S., W. J. Koch, and R. J. McNally. 1992. How does anxiety sensitivity vary across the anxiety disorders? *Journal of Anxiety Disorders* 6 (3):249–59.

Taylor, S., W. J. Koch, R. J. McNally, and D. J. Crockett. 1992. Conceptualizations of anxiety sensitivity. *Psychological Assessment* 4 (2):245–50.

Taylor, S., W. J. Koch, S. Woody, and P. McLean. 1996. Anxiety sensitivity and depression: How are they related? *Journal of Abnormal Psychology* 105 (3):474–79.

Teasdale, J. D., Z. V. Segal, J. M. G. Williams, V. A. Ridgeway, J. M. Soulsby, and M. A. Lau. 2000. Prevention of relapse/recurrence in major depression by mindfulness-based cognitive therapy. *Journal of Consulting and Clinical Psychology* 68 (4):615–23.

Telch, M. J., J. A. Lucas, and P. Nelson. 1989. Nonclinical panic in college students: An investigation of prevalence and symptomatology. *Journal of Abnormal Psychology* 98 (3):300–06.

Thorn, B. E., K. L. Clements, L. C. Ward, K. E. Dixon, B. C. Kersh, J. L. Boothby, and W. F. Chaplin. 2004. Personality factors in the explanation of sex differences in pain catastrophizing and response to experimental pain. *Clinical Journal of Pain* 20 (5):275–82.

Uman, L. S., S. H. Stewart, M. C. Watt, and A. Johnston. 2006. Differences in high and low anxiety sensitive women's responses to a laboratory-based cold pressor task. *Cognitive Behaviour Therapy* 35 (4):189–97.

U.S. Department of Health and Human Services and U.S. Department of Agriculture. 2005. *Dietary Guidelines for Americans*. Washington, DC: U.S. Government Printing Office (accessed May 15, 2008, at http://www.health.gov/DietaryGuidelines/dga2005/document/).

Vansteenwegen, D., T. Dirikx, D. Hermans, B. Vervliet, and P. Eelen. 2006. Renewal and reinstatement of fear: Evidence from human conditioning research. In *Fear and learning: From basic processes to clinical implications*, ed. M. G. Craske, D. Hermans, and D. Vansteenwegen. Washington, DC: American Psychological Association.

Varela, R. E., C. F. Weems, C. L. Berman, L. Hensley, and M. C. Rodriguez de Bernal. 2007. Internalizing symptoms in Latinos: The role of anxiety sensitivity. *Journal of Youth and Adolescence* 36:429–40.

Vriends, N., E. S. Becker, A. Meyer, S. L. Williams, R. Lutzc, and Jürgen Margraf. 2007. Recovery from social phobia in the community and its predictors: Data from a longitudinal epidemiological study. *Journal of Anxiety Disorders* 21 (3):320–37.

Wald, J. Forthcoming. A case study of interoceptive exposure therapy as a prelude to trauma-related exposure therapy in treating a PTSD patient with substantial comorbidity. *Journal of Cognitive Psychotherapy.*

Watson, J. B., and R. Rayner. 1920. Conditioned emotional reactions. *Journal of Experimental Psychology* 3 (1):1–14.

Watt, M. C. 2001. Age and gender differences in perception of control: Implications for development of anxious and dysphoric mood. *Dissertation Abstracts International, Section B: The Sciences and Engineering* 62 (2-B):1104.

Watt, M. C., C. D. Birch, S. H. Stewart, and D. B. Bernier. 2006. Brief CBT for high anxiety sensitivity decreases drinking and drinking problems: Evidence from a randomized controlled trial. *Journal of Mental Health* 15:683–95.

Watt, M. C., D. MacDonald, and L. Bilek. 2008. An investigation of anxiety sensitivity in a sample of varsity athletes. Working paper.

Watt, M. C., T. MacDonald, and M. J. Lefaivre. 2008. Anxiety sensitivity and physical activity: Gender differences in a non-clinical sample of adolescents. Working paper.

Watt, M. C., L. A. McWilliams, and A. G. Campbell. 2005. Relations between anxiety sensitivity and attachment style dimensions. *Journal of Psychopathology and Behavioral Assessment* 27 (3):191–200.

Watt, M. C., and S. H. Stewart. 2000. Anxiety sensitivity mediates the relationships between childhood learning experiences and elevated hypochondriacal concerns in young adulthood. *Journal of Psychosomatic Research* 49 (2):107–18.

Watt, M. C., S. H. Stewart, and D. B. Bernier. 2005. Reductions in depression scores following a brief cognitive-behavioural intervention targeting anxiety sensitivity. Paper presented at the 66th annual convention of the Canadian Psychological Association (CPA), June, in Montreal, Canada.

Watt, M. C., S. H. Stewart, C. D. Birch, and D. B. Bernier. 2006a. Brief CBT for high anxiety sensitivity decreases drinking problems [relieves] alcohol outcome expectancies and conformity drinking motives: Evidence from a randomized controlled trial. *Journal of Mental Health* 15 (6):683–95.

Watt, M. C., S. H. Stewart, P. J. Conrod, and N. B. Schmidt. 2008. Personality-based approaches to treatment of co-morbid anxiety and substance use disorder. In *Anxiety and substance use disorders: The vicious cycle of comorbidity*, ed. S. H. Stewart and P. J. Conrod, 201–19. New York: Springer Science and Business Media, LLC.

Watt, M. C., S. H. Stewart, and B. J. Cox. 1998. A retrospective study of the learning history origins of anxiety sensitivity. *Behaviour Research and Therapy* 36 (5):505–25.

Watt, M. C., S. Stewart, M. J. Lefaivre, and L. A. Uman. 2006b. Brief cognitive-behavioural approach to reducing anxiety sensitivity decreases anxiety related to pain. *Cognitive Behaviour Therapy* 35:248–56.

Weems, C. F., S. L. Berman, W. K. Silverman, and E. T. Rodriguez. 2002a. The relation between anxiety sensitivity and attachment style in adolesence and early adulthood. *Journal of Psychopathology and Behavioral Assessment* 24 (3):159–68.

Weems, C. F., C. Hayward, J. Killen, and C. B. Taylor. 2002b. A longitudinal investigation of anxiety sensitivity in adolescence. *Journal of Abnormal Psychology* 111 (3):471–77.

Westra, H. A., and D. J. A. Dozois. 2008. Integrating motivational interviewing into the treatment of anxiety. In *Motivational interviewing in the treatment of psychological problems*, ed. H. Arkowitz, H. A. Westra, W. R. Miller, and S. Rollnick. New York: The Guilford Press.

Wilson, M., D. Bell-Dolan, and B. Beitman. 1997. Application of the stages of change scale in a clinical drug trial. *Journal of Anxiety Disorders* 11 (4):395–408.

Winfield, I., L. K. George, M. Swartz, and D. G. Blazer. 1990. Sexual assault and psychiatric disorders among a community sample of women. *American Journal of Psychiatry* 147 (3):335–41.

Witkiewitz, K., and G. A. Marlatt. 2004. Relapse prevention for alcohol and drug problems: That was Zen, this is Tao. *American Psychologist* 59 (4):224–35.

Wittchen, H. U., M. B. Stein, and R. C. Kessler. 1999. Social fears and social phobia in a community sample of adolescents and young adults: Prevalence, risk factors and co-morbidity. *Psychological Medicine* 29 (2):309–23.

Yerkes, R. M., and J. D. Dodson. 1908. The relation of strength of stimulus to rapidity of habit-formation. *Journal of Comparative Neurology and Psychology* 18 (5):459–82.

Yovetich, N. A., J. A. Dale, and M. A. Hudak. 1990. Benefits of humor in reduction of threat-induced anxiety. *Psychological Reports* 66 (1):51–58.

Zahradnik, M., S. H. Stewart, D. Stevens, C. Wekerle, N. M. Comeau, and C. Mushquash. 2007. Creating a collaborative understanding of pathways to adolescent alcohol misuse in a Mi'kmaq community. Paper presented at symposium titled Critical Issues in the Development of Collaborative Culturally Relevant Early Intervention Approaches Targeting Aboriginal Youth Substance Abuse at the Issues of Substance (CCSA) Conference, November 25–28, in Edmonton, Alberta, Canada.

Zahradnik, M., S. H. Stewart, G. N. Marshall, T. L. Schell, and L. H. Jaycox. In press. Anxiety sensitivity and alexithymia are independently and uniquely associated with post-traumatic distress. *Journal of Traumatic Stress.*

Zimmerman, G. L., C. G. Olsen, and M. F. Bosworth. 2000. A "stages of change" approach to helping patients change behavior. *American Family Physician* 61 (5):1409–16.

Zinbarg, R. E., D. H. Barlow, and T. A. Brown. 1997. Hierarchical structure and general factor saturation of the anxiety sensitivity index: Evidence and implications. *Psychological Assessment* 9 (3):277–84.

Zvolensky, M. J., and A. Bernstein. 2005. Cigarette smoking and panic psychopathology. *Current Directions in Psychological Science* 14 (6):301–05.

Zvolensky, M. J., A. Bernstein, S. J. Cardenas, V. A. Colotla, E. C. Marshall, and M. T. Feldner. 2007. Anxiety sensitivity and early relapse to smoking: A test among Mexican daily, low-level smokers. *Nicotine and Tobacco Research* 9 (4):483–91.

Zvolensky, M. J., M. Bonn-Miller, A. Bernstein, and E. Marshall. 2006. Anxiety sensitivity and abstinence duration to smoking. *Journal of Mental Health* 15 (6):659–70.

Zvolensky, M. J., G. H. Eifert, and C. W. Lejuez. 2001. Offset control during recurrent 20% carbon dioxide-enriched air induction: Relation to individual difference variables. *Emotion* 1 (2):148–65.

Zvolensky, M. J., R. Kotov, A. V. Antipova, and N. B. Schmidt. 2005. Diathesis stress model for panic-related distress: A test in a Russian epidemiological sample. *Behaviour Research and Therapy* 43 (4):521–32.

Zvolensky, M. J., C. W. Lejuez, C. W. Kahler, and R. A. Brown. 2003. Integrating an interoceptive exposure-based smoking cessation program into the cognitive-behavioral treatment of panic disorder: Theoretical relevance and case demonstration. *Cognitive and Behavioral Practice* 10 (4):347–57.

Zvolensky, M. J., N. B. Schmidt, and S. H. Stewart. 2003. Panic disorder and smoking. *Clinical Psychology: Science and Practice* 10 (1):29–51.

Margo C. Watt, Ph.D., is associate professor of psychology at St. Francis Xavier University in Antigonish, NS, Canada, and adjunct professor of psychology at Dalhousie University in Halifax, NS, Canada. She is a licensed clinical psychologist in the province of Nova Scotia, where she maintains a limited private practice, and has training and experience in clinical, health, and forensic psychology. Her research is funded by the Social Sciences and Humanities Research Council and the Nova Scotia Health Research Foundation.

Sherry H. Stewart, Ph.D., is a Killam research professor in the Departments of Psychiatry, Psychology, and Community Health and Epidemiology at Dalhousie University in Halifax, NS, Canada. She is a licensed psychologist in the province of Nova Scotia. Her research focuses on risk factors for anxiety and the overlap of anxiety and addictive behaviors. She has received research funding from such agencies as the Canadian Institutes of Health Research, the National Institutes of Alcohol Abuse and Alcoholism, and the Alcoholic Beverage Medical Research Foundation.

Foreword writer **Steven Taylor, Ph.D.,** is professor of psychiatry at the University of British Columbia. He is author of *Anxiety Sensitivity*, the first textbook to review the research on assessment and treatment of anxiety sensitivity.

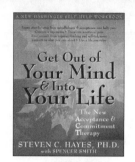
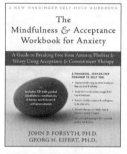
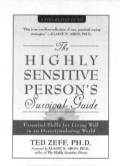

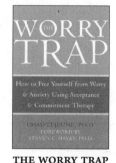